METAPHOR IN PUBLIC POLICY AND PRIVATE PRACTICE

A Social Work Perspective

GERALD V. O'BRIEN

NASW PRESS

National Association of Social Workers
Washington, DC

Kathryn Conley Wehrmann, PhD, MPH, ACSW, *President*
Angelo McClain, PhD, LCSW, *Chief Executive Officer*

Cheryl Y. Bradley, *Publisher*
Rachel Meyers, *Acquisitions Editor*
Julie Gutin, *Managing Editor*
Sarah Lowman, *Project Manager*
Kathleen P. Baker, *Copyeditor*
Julie Palmer-Hoffman, *Proofreader*
Matthew White, *Indexer*

Cover by Ashley Slade
Interior design, composition, and eBook conversions by Rick Soldin
Printed and bound by P. A. Hutchison Company

First impression: December 2019

© 2019 by the NASW Press

All rights reserved. No part of this book may be reproduced or transmitted in any form or by any means, electronic or mechanical, including photocopying, recording, or by any information storage and retrieval system, without permission in writing from the publisher.

Library of Congress Cataloging-in-Publication Data

Names: O'Brien, Gerald V., author.
Title: Metaphor analysis in public policy and private practice : a social
   work perspective / Gerald V. O'Brien.
Description: Washington, DC : NASW Press, National Association of Social
   Workers, [2019] | Includes bibliographical references and index. |
   Summary: "The book focuses on the impact of metaphor analysis on social
   policy and makes the case that students cannot be effective policy
   advocates unless they develop a good understanding of metaphor framing.
   The book describes the potential importance of metaphor awareness for
   practitioners"—Provided by publisher.
Identifiers: LCCN 2019028786 | ISBN 9780871015488 (paperback) | ISBN
   9780871015495 (epub)
Subjects: LCSH: Public policy. | Metaphor. | Social service.
Classification: LCC H97 .O323 2019 | DDC 320.601/4—dc23
LC record available at https://lccn.loc.gov/2019028786

Printed in the United States of America

Dedicated with love to my wife, Jean, and to Kevin, Mark, Shannon, Jade, Quinn, and Willow

CONTENTS

About the Author vii

Acknowledgments ix

Introduction 1

CHAPTER 1 Metaphors and the Social Work Profession:
A Brief Overview 9

CHAPTER 2 Metaphors and Denigration: Social Justice
Implications 25

CHAPTER 3 Metaphors and Social Welfare Policy 41

CHAPTER 4 Metaphors That Dehumanize and Objectify 55

CHAPTER 5 Metaphors That Evoke Threat and
Fear Responses 81

CHAPTER 6 Implications for Social Work Study,
Practice, and Policy Advocacy 99

Conclusion 109

References 111

Index 133

ABOUT THE AUTHOR

Gerald (Jerry) V. O'Brien, PhD, is a professor in the Social Work Department at Southern Illinois University Edwardsville, where he has taught for the past two decades. He received his BSW from the University of Missouri–St. Louis, his MSW from the University of Missouri–Columbia, and his PhD from the University of Illinois at Urbana–Champaign.

Dr. O'Brien teaches classes in community organizing, policy analysis, research and disability studies at both the undergraduate and the graduate level. His research focuses on disability history and policy, with particular emphasis on eugenics, as well as metaphor analysis in relation to social injustice and stigmatization. His articles have been published in *Social Work*, the *Journal of Social Work Education*, the *Journal of Sociology and Social Welfare*, *Metaphor and Symbol*, and other journals. This is his third book, following *Framing the Moron: The Social Construction of Feeble-Mindedness in the American Eugenic Era* (Manchester University Press, 2013) and *Contagion and the National Body: The Organism Metaphor in American Thought* (Routledge, 2018).

ACKNOWLEDGMENTS

I first thank my colleagues in the Department of Social Work and College of Arts and Sciences at Southern Illinois University Edwardsville. They have been very supportive of my research over the years. My fields of study—historical analysis, eugenics, and metaphor analysis—are a bit off the beaten track for a social work scholar, but I have never been dissuaded from engaging in forms of scholarly activity that I believe are important to the field and to social work education. I am also grateful to all the students I have had over the years, especially in the many policy classes I have taught. I have learned a great deal about social policy from my engagement with these students, and I am particularly pleased when I find that alumni are continuing to invest themselves in policy advocacy on behalf of their clients and their agencies.

I came to metaphor analysis through a circuitous route, and I am grateful to those scholars whose writings have guided me along the way. These scholars include George Lakoff, Sam Keen, Martha Nussbaum, Lise Noël, Sander Gilman, Mark Landau, Andreas Musolff, Jonathon Charteris-Black, Mary Douglas, Otto Santa Ana, and Paul Rozin. I am also appreciative of the following social work scholars for their policy or metaphor research that has influenced me: Vicki Lens, Eileen Gambrill, Bruce Jansson, and Yoosun Park. Thanks also to Jim Trent, who has had an important influence on my research, as well as my friends in the disability studies community, particularly my fellow eugenics and disability scholars who accompanied me on a month-long seminar in Germany in 2004. They and this experience contributed greatly to my understanding of social justice and the rhetorical mechanisms supporting dehumanization and oppression.

This book is an extension of a 2009 article that I wrote titled "Metaphors and the Pejorative Framing of Marginalized Groups: Implications for Social Work Education." This article was published in the *Journal of Social Work Education,* and I am grateful that they have granted permission for me to use revised sections of the article in this book. Thanks to everyone at NASW Press, especially Rachel Meyers, and to the reviewers of the draft, who provided very helpful feedback on revisions and recommendations for additional source material.

Finally, I want to take this opportunity to state how grateful I am to my family. My wife, Jean, has always been extremely supportive of my work even though it often takes me away from other, more important things. Thanks to my children, Kevin, Mark, and Shannon, as well as to Jade and Quinn. Thanks also to my extended family, and especially my parents and my wife's parents. I have had incredible support over the years and am grateful to everyone who has expressed an interest in my work.

INTRODUCTION

Policy advocacy has become a central component of both the social work field and higher education in the profession. Not only does public policy at multiple levels (international, federal, state, county, local) have tremendous influence on the range and quality of the services offered by social workers, but the most important route to social justice is also often through effective engagement in the policy arena. Moreover, policy advocacy cannot simply be the domain of experts in the area; it is the responsibility of all social workers and others who consider themselves allies for social justice matters. In the following chapters, I attempt to provide justification for this position. Although most professionals will not specialize in policy practice, all must be capable of navigating these waters when the need arises. Fear, anxiety, or frustration regarding such intervention is unacceptable if social workers are to work as best they can on behalf of their clients and live up to the profession's code of ethics.

Most would agree that the profession currently faces unparalleled challenges in the assessment of social problems and in the development and implementation of social policies related to them. The nation seems to be increasingly divided, and people are constantly talking across one another—invoking different "policy languages," one might say (Bishop, 2008; Haidt, 2012; Lakoff, 1996). Partisans on each side of the political divide often feel that what appears perfectly logical and obvious to them makes no sense to those on the other side. Rising frustration and anger, intensified by the chronic use of social media and other platforms that are not conducive to constructive civil discourse, lead many to want to simply withdraw from the debate altogether. At the same time, people are inundated with policy-related information and propaganda and have difficulty telling the difference between the two. They also do not have the luxury to explore complex social issues in the depth that they deserve.

Perhaps most important, policy making is ostensibly an emotional enterprise, but people experience frustration because they falsely believe that it is governed by reason, and they fail to understand why rational arguments and facts do not carry the day. Moreover, even what seems to constitute a fact is today increasingly and purposefully obscured by various political stakeholders to press their personal narratives.

My hope is that, among other things, this book will provide cogent reasons why practicing social workers, professors, students, clients, and others who consider themselves to be allies for social justice concerns should not move to the political sidelines out of frustration but should rather take a more active role in policy engagement. The more one understands political systems and how they affect the social services network as a whole, the greater comfort one will have working in an environment that at first appears alien and perhaps even manifestly corrupt. This landscape is discomforting to many people for various reasons, but the negative attributes of the political system, and there are surely many, are not an excuse to refrain from engagement. This political system, imperfect as it may be, is the only one this country has. Despite its flaws, it is also a system that will occasionally greatly benefit those in need or, conversely, add to their struggles.

The primary point of this book is that social workers must not only be involved in the policy arena, but should especially be aware of and engaged in problem framing. I contend that this initial stage of the policy-making process is by far the most important one, because framing drives which social policies and therefore social services are developed and maintained. A key component of social problem analysis is metaphoric framing: understanding how language (as well as images) is used to describe a particular social problem. As I emphasize in this book, language is weighty, in that even what appear to be superficial rhetorical differences can dramatically change the way people feel about a problem and therefore the potential policy responses and services that are supported. Especially in the policy arena, language is also purposeful, with specific terms, images, events, and stories being purposefully used to present a desired picture of the social problem. This picture, moreover, serves specific stakeholder interests and is designed to funnel money and resources down prearranged pathways.

The endpoint of these funding pathways is where these decisions primarily affect social workers. Which pathway is selected explains why some services are funded more readily than others; why some clients have greater access than others; why some treatments are more favored than others; and why some agencies or services develop, expand, or fail to thrive. Problem framing is of vital importance in what social workers do. In addition, framing also has an impact on the social work profession and the public sanction that is (or is not) provided in support of the profession. Social workers are left with two choices: either adapt to the existing problem–policy pathway or be engaged in the process of attempting to change it. Not only does the former option mean relegating oneself to a particular service delivery typology, but it may even require an uncomfortable adaptation of one's values and ethical beliefs, because varying service delivery typologies may carry with them differing views of both problem etiology and the theoretical approach to the issue or treatment. Certain policy pathways carry with them the inherent perspective that marginalized individuals are to blame for their condition, and others place greater blame on the larger systems within which those individuals live.

As many readers can no doubt surmise, metaphoric framing stands as a form of social constructionism. The meaning of particular terms and images is not fixed, but changes on the basis of cultural and historical circumstances (Burr, 1995). As Gergen (1999) wrote, being able to deconstruct language has emancipatory potential because it opens to people new vistas for understanding. He added that "there is substantial work on the ways discourse is subtly used to maintain power relations, to derogate certain groups of people, and to silence those who might upset the status quo" (p. 80). Changing one's metaphors and the way in which groups, problems, or policies are described and conceptually understood is perhaps the best way to augment dialogue with those who view issues from a different perspective. Social work educators frequently discuss the importance of using multiple perspectives in conceptualizing issues. Drawing on different metaphors can assist educators in gaining this new perspective. Moreover, understanding metaphors can allow one to grasp more fully why one holds a perspective on a particular issue.

Although this book focuses specifically on linguistic and conceptual metaphors, I should note that a variety of communication vehicles may carry metaphoric meaning and support or oppose particular framings (Indurkhya, 1992). Images and photographs, for example, are often designed with metaphoric intent. In his book *Faces of the Enemy,* Sam Keen (1986) provided a description of the ways in which war posters have been designed to support entrenched, dehumanizing views of the enemy during wartime, and Garland-Thomson (2001), in her book chapter "Seeing the Disabled," provided both positive and negative examples of visual images as modes of framing people with disabilities. In two of his books, Sander Gilman (1984, 1988) provided insight into how, over the course of time, mental illness has been depicted through various types of images. In his book *Seeing Through Race: A Reinterpretation of Civil Rights Photography,* Martin Berger (2011) not only described the importance of photography in the context of the civil rights movement, but moreover analyzed which particular depictions were "acceptable" to different audiences, and therefore which framings of protests were likely to be widely disseminated, usually because they fostered the existing narrative of the media source or region. Often, as one might assume, verbal and pictorial descriptions have worked together in fostering a particular frame.

As I describe in chapter 2, select themes have been used over time for the purpose of dehumanizing or inciting fear of marginalized community groups. These themes are often recycled in different eras and generally work in a largely subliminal manner. Periods that are marked by dehumanizing and fear-based rhetoric are also characterized by efforts to formally or informally limit the rights of such groups. Formal methods of restriction will normally be at the level of social policy. As alluded to earlier, because these periods of dehumanization are marked by high emotion (anger, fear, anxiety), they are not highly responsive to rational arguments in support of the oppressed group. Rather, social workers need to understand why specific metaphoric themes are being used and make the public cognizant of them. We need to shed light on political manipulation and how (and why) it works, especially when the rights or even lives of vulnerable groups may be at risk.

ORGANIZATION OF THE TEXT

This book consists of two sections. The first three chapters provide an overview of metaphoric themes and their importance in social policy. Chapter 1 includes a brief literature review of metaphors in social work. Previous published works in social work and related fields have almost exclusively dealt with the use of metaphor in the context of clinical practice, with very little being written about the relationship between metaphors and public policy. As I describe in chapter 3, however, this has been a burgeoning area of research outside of the profession. Understanding the use of metaphor analysis in clinical practice is beneficial because it informs metaphoric deconstruction in regard to policy, and vice versa. In both domains, social workers must be aware that metaphors can tell one much about what is being communicated and why.

The second chapter specifically takes up two related issues. First, I look at research, much of it fairly recent, into how metaphors may affect, even subconsciously, the way that people think about and respond to social issues and make decisions related to them. Not only do metaphors play an integral role in decision making, but they may also reveal much about implicit bias. Second, I take up the relationship between pejorative metaphor themes and devalued subgroups and explore how various linguistic and conceptual metaphors have been used to denigrate specific groups. This discussion sets the stage for the more in-depth discussion provided in chapters 4 and 5. I also discuss the issue of metaphoric themes in relation to the public image of the social work profession itself.

In chapter 3, I consider in greater depth the relationship between metaphors and public policy and the importance of this form of policy advocacy for the social work profession. As alluded to earlier, the past few decades have seen an explosion of research demonstrating the relationship between various metaphor themes and public policies. This topic is especially important because many of the issues that social workers deal with are emotionally charged, and therefore stakeholders are likely to invoke metaphors that have a subconscious emotional impact.

In the second section of this book, chapters 4 and 5 provide more detailed examples of metaphor themes as they have been used over time to denigrate vulnerable populations and support restrictive social policies. In chapter 4, I focus on dehumanization and objectification themes, and in chapter 5 I highlight fear-based rhetoric and images. Both historical and contemporary examples are used, and for the former I principally use primary source writings from alarm periods. Although most of the examples are from the United States, I periodically pull in some from other nations, particularly Nazi Germany. The use of denigrating metaphors in the Nazi era is important in part because to a large extent dehumanizing propaganda became institutionalized in Nazi Germany. Although negative verbal and pictorial depictions of marginalized groups have been used for centuries, Hitler, in conjunction with leading Nazis such as Joseph Goebbels, Heinrich Himmler, Alfred Rosenberg, and Julius Streicher, was the first to create a vast propaganda infrastructure to support his measures of control and extermination (Burleigh, 1994).

Although most of the historical examples I draw from (for example, immigration restriction, anti-Semitism, racial segregation, Japanese internment) are generally well known to readers, one period of social injustice I highlight that I should briefly explain is the eugenics movement in the United States. This movement, which peaked during the 1920s, held that the nation could become stronger by controlling reproduction, especially by limiting births among the least desirable elements of the population. These groups, many of whom were diagnosed as feebleminded or morons, presumably had large numbers of children and threatened to overwhelm the nation (Kennedy, 2008; O'Brien, 2018; Trent, 1994). Eugenicists contended that, together with undesirable immigrant groups, these people also threatened to dilute the racial makeup of the nation. As a result of these and other arguments, policies such as involuntary sterilization and forced institutionalization laws were passed in many states to control the birth rate among such people (Reilly, 1991). As one might assume, the U.S. eugenics era informed later Nazi eugenics policies. Important for the purposes of this book, similar forms of image making took place in each nation to dehumanize people with disabilities and other victims of eugenics policies (Kühl, 1994; O'Brien, 2013).

The brief final chapter of the book details implications of this work for the social work community. It addresses the inclusion of metaphoric content not only in policy, but also in research, diversity, and practice courses; the role of social workers as policy advocates; and short-term policy challenges for the profession. I also briefly discuss important ethical considerations related to metaphor analysis. For example, although one might assume that a response to pejorative metaphors would be to replace them with more positive metaphors, this can be problematic because even the latter generally constitute stereotyping.

My hope is that this book will provide readers with greater insight into the meaning behind people's words, as well as the ways in which conceptual metaphors guide people's thinking. Over the past decade, many in the social work profession have, like other Americans, become greatly concerned about the state of the nation's politics, as well as trends such as the growing political divide, negative campaigning, and the infusion of ever more corporate money into politics. Instead of allowing these and other disconcerting political developments to drive people away from politics, countervailing winds provide hope for the future. Many people are becoming increasingly engaged and taking part in activist campaigns. Although there are certainly drawbacks to social media, they have, in an age of mass media homogeneity, allowed many smaller voices to make themselves heard and allowed for a multitude of opinions. Many young people are coming to understand the importance of being engaged (such as by voting) to shape the future. Just as social workers have an interest in the strengths perspective when viewing client issues, they need to focus on positive trends that can be found in the intersection of politics and social work and find ways to take advantage of and expand on these positive trends. Perhaps the metaphors that are implicitly drawn from framing policy practice themselves need to be changed.

1
Metaphors and the Social Work Profession: A Brief Overview

Finding the right word is as important as finding the right evidence.
—Lens (2005, p. 234)

Since people think in metaphors, the key to understanding human thought is to deconstruct those metaphors.
—Pinker (2008, p. 238)

The word "metaphor" derives from the Greek word *metaphora,* which means to change the location of something (*meta*) from one place to another by moving or carrying it (*phor*) (Gould, 1995). According to Donald Schön (1979), "Metaphorical utterances" constitute "the 'carrying over' of frames or perspectives from one domain of experience to another" (p. 254). In the pages that follow, I describe the various ways in which negative perspectives or feelings, often presented in the guise of specific metaphor themes or disgust-laden phenomena, are carried over to and have an adverse impact on marginalized populations and serve to reinforce the development of public policy initiatives that act in opposition to and seek to control or disparage such groups. As I argue, this information is essential for social workers and other allies for social justice to understand if they are to adequately engage in their role as advocates for both vulnerable and oppressed groups and the profession itself. Effective engagement in the policy arena to support the profession's goals requires a basic understanding of metaphors.

OVERVIEW OF METAPHORS AND THEIR IMPORTANCE

At their most basic level, metaphors include both a source and a target domain.[1] In the case of the frequently used welfare-recipient-as-parasite metaphor, for example, the parasite constitutes the source domain, and welfare recipient constitutes the target. The primary rationale for the metaphor is to carry over, or transfer, important although often covert aspects of the source entity (for example, dependence, weakness, laziness, low or diminished status, potential to harm the host or contaminate others) to the target. One of the reasons that the welfare-recipient-as-parasite metaphor is so potent is surely because in the popular imagination they reside together. Parasites and disease have always been associated with those who live in tenements, ghettoes, asylums, and other spaces that are associated with abject poverty. Not only has disease long been associated with poverty and foreignness, but moreover, these target groups are presumed to be responsible for both causing and spreading, rather than being victimized by, such parasites and diseases (Goatly, 2007). It is not reaching too far to say that in the popular imagination, metaphorical human parasites (homeless people, welfare recipients, people with certain disabilities) are perceived to be a vector through which real parasites connect to or threaten to invade the normal population.

To quote Susan Sontag (1990), "Saying a thing is or is like something-it-is-not is a mental operation as old as philosophy and poetry, and the spawning ground of most kinds of understanding, including scientific understanding, and expressiveness" (p. 93). Others have written that metaphors are the means by which societies build "webs of collective meaning" (Harrington, 1995) and that the "ultimate way to extend one's perspective to others is through metaphor" (Ellwood, 1995, p. 93). Although many would contend that metaphors simply constitute a novel or interesting way of describing something that has little real impact on how people think or respond to issues, an accumulation of evidence stands in contrast to this contention and demonstrates metaphors' important although often subliminal impact. As Lee and Schwartz (2013) wrote, "A rapidly growing body of experimental research provides persuasive evidence

---

[1] A version of some of the content in this section was previously published in O'Brien (2009).

Metaphors and the Social Work Profession

for the role of metaphors in human thought" (p. 86). This is obviously important because how people think about issues has a direct impact on how they respond to them, including through public policies. I return to and expand on this issue in chapter 2.

The connection of source and target domains "through metaphor can affect the way that those domains are understood, causing the perceived similarity of members of the two domains to increase" (Allbritton, 1995, p. 36). Along with others, George Lakoff (1995), a leading contemporary metaphor analyst and scholar, contended that it is virtually impossible for people to think without the automatic subconscious assistance of metaphors, and metaphors therefore play a crucial role in how people understand the world around them. One reason for this is that people develop an awareness of new or unfamiliar phenomena on the basis of what they already know, often through metaphoric connections.

In complex fields of study whose many intricacies are beyond most people's understanding, experts or commentators will use concrete, real-world examples to explain important research findings, hypotheses, or new developments (Ringmar, 2008). Thus, complicated medical or genetic advancements are often described to the general public through the medium of metaphoric analogies (Boone, 1988). The Human Genome Project, for example, may be described as a search for the Holy Grail of human essence (Nelkin & Tancredi, 1989), or HIV may be framed as a Trojan horse virus or time bomb that invades the body and silently waits until the right time to strike. Many professors in social work as well as in other professions certainly try to find metaphors that can serve as a bridge to what may be challenging cognitive terrain for students.

How People Respond to Metaphors

As noted earlier, metaphors not only may provide meaning about the alleged "essence" of a thing, person, or group, but also may carry covert or overt messages about the recommended modes of treating or responding to the target or targets (Schön, 1979). If welfare recipients are parasites, their segregation from the mainstream community is likely to be maintained. People may develop methods of marking such individuals, as well as a system of surveillance, and find ways to control their movements within the community. They may also take action to ensure that these individuals will not propagate and spread. The response to such people, in short, may be akin to a form of sanitation control or preventive public health.[2] As Kövecses (2010) noted, metaphors are generally unidirectional, in that the source domain affects people's beliefs about the target, but not the other way around. In other words, drawing on the preceding example, people's revulsion toward parasites may adversely influence how they respond to welfare recipients, but welfare recipients' attributes are not going to be used to frame how people view parasites.

An important theme in this book is that a particular metaphor's impact on policy and thus the way in which the funding and service pathway is framed is especially important in whether one attributes an individual or a systemic or environmental cause to particular problems and thus where the focus for change (or implied blame) lies. The parasite metaphor related to welfare, homelessness, and poverty implies that individuals are at fault for their conditions. Parasites are not expected or even capable of change; they (and their progeny) are what they were born to be. All that is important is that they not threaten the mass of the population, that they stay in their place. Policies that inadvertently support their spread are viewed as inimical to community health. A differing metaphor that would carry with it assumptions about systemic rather than individual dysfunction is the mechanical metaphor, in which society is seen as a machine that has simply stopped functioning in certain ways, and various groups are adversely affected by the breakdown of the machinery—caught in the gears, so to speak.

Conceptual Metaphors

In addition to linguistic metaphors, scholars frequently point out the importance of more broad conceptual metaphors. A conceptual metaphor relates not just to a metaphorical term, phrase, or image but to a more global way of thinking about a particular object, person or people, group, or social problem (Allbritton, 1995). Many scholars have described conceptual metaphors as a form of mapping (Landau &

---

[2] To provide one example, sterilizing people with intellectual disabilities, welfare recipients, or other undesirable segments of the population has been described by some scholars as akin to other forms of sterilization (for example, of medical instruments)—as a method of ensuring that contagious diseases will not spread. It is not completely surprising that an early term for "genes" was "germ plasm." In a sense, genes, and particularly bad genes, were viewed as potentially contaminating entities during the eugenics era because they carried adverse characteristics from parents to their children (Pernick, 1996). Anyone who inadvertently mated with a representative of such a family was also apt to find their own blood (as well as that of their descendants) contaminated.

Keefer, 2014). If, for example, welfare recipients are viewed as parasites, one can consider the various characteristics that seem to typify both the source and the target entities and specifically identify and focus on those characteristics or traits that most closely relate to both domains. As the connection between the source and target domain is solidified and becomes part of people's belief system, they subconsciously selectively take note of and incorporate those characterological elements that connect the two. People are additionally drawn to and find comfort in those media sources, authorities, stories, and modes of presentation that support their pre-existing metaphoric framings. Questioning prevailing metaphors may lead to fear and anxiety because they may be part of an interconnected web of meaning that tells people much about the nature of the world and their role in it.

Metaphors can even be reified, or made to appear real, through social actions that formalize the connection between the source and target domains (Harper & Raman, 2008; O'Brien, 2010). For example, although Jews were metaphorically viewed as parasites and contagious entities in Nazi Germany, this metaphor was reified when they were placed in disease environs. In some Nazi writing from the Holocaust, it is almost difficult to tell whether certain descriptors of contaminating Jews were metaphoric or not.[3] Indeed, such obscurity was the point because the writers implicitly understood that the conflation of the metaphoric with reality would ensure that the metaphoric image would be more willingly accepted by the public. Because of the frequent use of contagion-laced images, German citizens realized that, for their own protection, if for no other reason, they should treat Jews as if they indeed carried a transmissible disease or lice. Even those people who might have Jewish blood but who identified themselves as Aryan were to be avoided in the same way in which one might refrain from contact with an asymptomatic carrier of disease.

A related example is the McCarthy-era view of Communism. Over time, the Communist net was increasingly widened to include not only those who had been involved in targeted groups or activities, but even individuals with whom they came into contact. Communism itself came

---

[3] As I further discuss in chapter 5, contagion metaphors related to Jews were a central metaphor theme of *Mein Kampf* (Hitler, 1971), written almost a decade before Hitler was elected into office. They became particularly important during the Third Reich, however, as the state-as-body-or-physical-organism metaphor came to be embraced as a central conceptual theme undergirding Nazi rule (Harrington, 1995; Musolff, 2007).

to be viewed as a form of contagion, in large part because anti-Communist writings were rife with contagion metaphors. In a 1954 article published in *Vital Speeches of the Day,* former President Herbert Hoover provided a range of such metaphors. He described, for example, the "bloody virus type" of Communism that "is today rotting the souls of two-fifths of all mankind" (p. 681). He deplored the "poison gas" spread by "fuzzy-minded intellectuals" and noted that "only a drop of typhoid in a barrel of drinking water sickens a whole village" (p. 681).[4]

Metaphors and Social Policy Development

The primary goal of this book is to point out to social workers and other allies for social justice the importance of metaphoric patterns in how political stakeholders and the public at large respond to marginalized groups, particularly through social policy development. I argue that advocacy for oppressed populations, which is a key element of social work, dictates that social workers become capable of analyzing or deconstructing harmful metaphoric patterns, understand how these metaphors support demeaning stereotypes, and strive to shed light on why such images are often so effective in creating a specific perceptual image of these devalued community subgroups. To reiterate a crucial point, these shared public images do not influence just public policy and public relations. Because these images support specific response options over others, they have a real-world impact on the direction taken by social service agencies and the service opportunities that are allowed to develop. The creation, maintenance, evolution, or even destruction of certain agencies or service funding streams, then, is directly related to these problem and response framings. Those social service agencies or jobs that are most likely to be funded will be those that are most in line with the existing metaphoric or framing pathway.[5]

I return to this issue in the forthcoming chapters. In the remainder of this introductory chapter, however, I take up the issue of metaphors as they have been used in social work and related fields of practice.

---

[4]The perception that Communism was akin to a communicable disease was certainly supported in part by the efforts that were made during the McCarthy era to connect Communism to homosexuality; even long before the HIV scare, religious leaders and others conceptually connected male homosexuality to the spread of disease.

[5]Many examples of this are found in the literature. A few good ones are Annas (1995), who reviewed the impact of health care metaphors on health policy, and Ellwood (1995), who described the framing of the War on Drugs. I share additional examples throughout the book.

Although little has been written in the profession about the importance of metaphor analysis for policy advocacy, metaphors have long had a central place in the profession in their support of both client assessment and therapeutic treatment.

METAPHORS AND SOCIAL WORK: A BRIEF LITERATURE REVIEW

Although some social work writings have described the potential importance of metaphor analysis in the profession, few of these works have touched on policy and the related social justice considerations. Normally, metaphor is discussed as a useful tool for micro- or meso-level clinical intervention because "metaphoric language has been an important therapeutic tool since the first counselor attempted to understand fully a client's experience of the world" (Wickman, Daniels, White, & Fesmire, 1999, p. 389). As Fox (1989) wrote, metaphors "are indispensable sources of information and guidance for both diagnosis and treatment" (p. 233). Articles by M. V. Adams (1997) and Lyddon, Clay, and Sparks (2001) provide examples of metaphors as a fruitful means of providing clients with increased awareness of their issues, as an unusual but potentially beneficial method of soliciting difficult information from individuals or, as Lyddon et al. noted, for "introducing new frames of reference" from which clients can consider their issues or goals. T. K. Duffy (2001) delineated various means of using metaphors to facilitate group work, and Amy Wilder (2004) discussed the importance of metaphors as an instructive way to understand group practice, focusing specifically on the metaphor of the human body as descriptive of group functioning.

As several of these writers have discussed, clients often draw on metaphors when making judgments about the issues that have led them to seek assistance from a social worker. The problems that couples may have, for example, often surround differences in the metaphors they use to view the world or their relationship (Wickman et al., 1999). Goldstein (1999) wrote that human problems "are not comprised of literal, objective facts" but rather are constructed in part "by metaphors that represent the way people think, reason, remember and talk about themselves" (p. 385). An example of this is the use of what I refer to as the "linear metaphor," whereby people judge themselves and their accomplishments (their goals, homes, cars, jobs, income, spouses, children, and so on) in comparison with others.

Especially in a highly competitive capitalist society, people are patterned to focus on conceptualizations of higher and lower, and they tend to move through their lives with an invisible measuring stick as their guide.

One should note, however, that metaphors are not just important in people's conscious efforts to make sense of the world and their individual situations. M. V. Adams (1997), for one, contended that the unconscious "is structured in and through metaphors" (p. 36). Many metaphors, as I show later, are designed to work in a largely subliminal fashion, particularly in the policy arena.

USING METAPHORS IN THERAPY

In his book *Metaphor Therapy,* Richard Kopp (1995) described in detail how clinicians can use metaphors in therapy. He said that although metaphors are a beneficial means of having clients discuss difficult issues in a symbolic or indirect manner, clinicians should not be highly purposeful in guiding clients. They might ask probing questions to pull out or expand on a metaphor, but the metaphor itself, as well as the meaning it holds, should normally be under the client's control. For example, if a client feels like she is in a pit or surrounded by a brick wall, she should be the one to describe the specific elements of this image and expand on it if need be. Sana Loue (2008) wrote that "clients can assume ownership and take their metaphors with them upon leaving therapy" (p. 134), as a touchstone. A metaphor that the client develops can form an entry point from which that client can further describe her or his situation and perhaps even develop possible response options.

Stott, Mansell, Salkovskis, Lavendar, and Cartwright-Hatton (2010) added that metaphors are particularly beneficial in counseling because clients often view their situation through a distorting lens, and metaphors may provide a novel, concrete means of perceiving their situation that might bring a degree of clarity. Stott et al. added that some of the most well-respected psychotherapists considered metaphors to be instrumental features of their clinical toolbox. The American therapist Milton Erickson (as cited in Stott et al., 2010) focused on metaphors as a means of activating "meaning in his clients at an implicit . . . level" (p. 12), and metaphoric images and words were a particularly important element of early psychoanalysis (see also Haley, 1973; Lyness & Thomas, 1995; Wickman et al., 1999). Both Freud and Jung were highly motivated by image metaphors, which were a seminal component of dream analysis (Fox, 1989;

Jung, 1964). M. V. Adams (1997) wrote that Freudian psychotherapy itself can be viewed as an example of the archeology metaphor, whereby the psychiatrist engages in a symbolic "excavation of buried ruins" that exists in clients' minds. Leary (1990) added that "a taxonomist would have to work long and hard to classify Freud's many metaphors" (p. 18).

Image- and Story-Based Metaphors

Word metaphors are an important component of word association tests, as are image metaphors in such assessment tools as the Rorschach Test. Image-based metaphors are a particularly crucial aspect of art therapy; family sculpting; sand, play, and puppet therapy; and other approaches that are designed to indirectly solicit information when openly innervating traumatic experiences is not the preferred method, particularly in work with children and adolescents or with adults recovering from trauma (Lyness & Thomas, 1995; Palmer, 2002).

Art therapist Shirley Riley (1999) wrote that "adolescents are constantly using their own individualized metaphors" and that "metaphor is another aspect of their creativity applied to communication" (p. 44). David Crenshaw (2006) added that "the power of symbol to evoke images for healing is the common thread that runs through all creative arts therapies" (p. 32). Saari (1986) contended that adolescents may particularly benefit from metaphor-related therapy because they may be "too old for play therapy and yet they are not truly capable of dealing with their problems purely through a direct discussion as is expected of adults" (p. 18).

Yet another way to indirectly solicit information in therapy with children is to use the metaphors contained in animal stories or fairy tales as prompts (Bettelheim, 1976; Combs & Freedman, 1990; Williams, 1995). Whether they pertain to images or words, metaphors are also important in narrative therapy, where they may allow clients to put a particular face on their feelings or situation and provide concrete examples that describe their feelings, hopes, or fears (Rutten, Mottart, & Soetaert, 2010). Ceremonies such as family rituals or certain family artifacts[6] may also serve as important metaphors for some clients (Combs & Freedman, 1990), and shared family metaphors may "serve as repositories of family experience and as guides for behavior" (Fox, 1989, p. 238).

---

[6]Family Bibles, for example, often carry a special significance not only because of their nature as a sacred text, but also because they may include family ancestral trees or other important family information.

Using Analogies in Therapy

Metaphors may allow individuals to provide explanations of their struggles or feelings by drawing on comfortable analogies, thus remaining in cognitive territory where they feel at home and in some control. A golfer who feels as though she is stuck in a rut and going nowhere may say she is in a sand trap, continually swinging at the ball but not moving on; a swimmer may feel like he is tethered to the side of the pool; a car dealer may feel as though he keeps trying to make the sale, but it never happens; and so forth. These examples can not only provide a viable mode of describing a situation, but also serve as potential areas for probing; in some cases, they may even provide some direction for resolving important dilemmas (Kopp, 1995). Hauser and Schwartz (2015) noted that metaphors "can affect the amount of message elaboration when they link the target to a domain that is of interest" (p. 67) to the client. In other words, if the clinician is aware of a particular interest of the client, the clinician can attempt to find ways to use analogies from that domain to assist in the treatment process.

An interesting form of therapy from Great Britain drew heavily on football (soccer to most of us who live in the United States) as a means of not only drawing men into therapy, but also providing a conceptual foundation for describing the various elements of the helping process. Men who were otherwise averse to talk therapy were able to bond over discussions that tacked back and forth between soccer and their own issues or problems and used a series of athletic metaphors to discuss their situations. The group was constituted as a team, with all members assisting each other and drawing on their own personal strengths to support goals. Lay leaders were not therapists but coaches, and sessions were referred to as "matches." The metaphor was even used spatially, because the group met in a stadium (Spandler, Roy, & Mckeown, 2014).

USE OF METAPHORS TO DECONSTRUCT COMPLEX ISSUES

Using metaphors to support a connection with or to empower clients may be particularly important when the social worker and client have radically different histories or experiences. Maria Zuñiga (1992) wrote that metaphors can be beneficial in the context of culturally competent practice. Especially when clients may have a different ethnic, demographic, or cultural background than the therapist, metaphors and sayings that are endemic to the client's culture may not only allow that client to express feelings and thoughts, but also assist the social worker in better understanding that culture and its value system, history, and traditions. Certain metaphors can also be used to provide shared meaning across different cultures.

Social workers use broad metaphors to make sense of the world, and they thus play an important role in assessment and treatment. Walter L. Miller (1980) discussed the central role of the medical model in social work, wherein professionals have carried over methods of diagnostics and treatment from the medical professions. As he noted, this way of perceiving the world, and individual and family issues, carries with it a wealth of potential problems. It is particularly instructive that this view has, as one might assume, especially been used in areas of social work that closely relate to medicine and rehabilitation.

Many disability scholars have discussed the anger and hurt that people with disabilities often feel in their relationships with social workers as a result of the latter's use of the medical model, which tends to focus heavily on deficits and the disempowerment of patients because of their presumed incapacities (Longmore & Umansky, 2001; Mackelprang & Salsgiver, 2015). Disability itself has a great many metaphoric undertones, and the assumptions that professionals often have regarding how disability should be framed are often at odds with how it is perceived by those who are directly affected (Lane, 1992). Indeed, it could be beneficial to compare a social worker's metaphor for the helping relationship with clients as a way of comparing their respective views of the treatment process and goals. An involuntary client, for example, may view the process from the perspective of the military metaphor, as a battle against the social worker. The challenge for the social worker might be to find a more productive metaphor as a mode of framing the relationship.

Journey Metaphor

Goldstein (1999) described root metaphors as basic truths about the world as social workers see it that inform their interactions with clients. As alluded to in some of the preceding examples, the nature of clinical social work means that certain broad metaphor themes are particularly apropos to the work engaged in by clinical social workers. One of these themes is the journey metaphor, whereby the client is viewed as being on a search or quest, with the social worker as a temporary guide who can assist in finding and interpreting clues that will help lead the client in the right direction or as a traveler with some previous knowledge of the terrain. The journey metaphor, with the client in the role of seeker and the worker in the role of guide, is much more humanizing than, for example, the mechanistic metaphor, in which the client is in need of fixing by the therapist or technician.

It is interesting that politicians also frequently invoke the journey metaphor for their own purposes. What Charteris-Black (2011) wrote in his book *Politicians and Rhetoric* could apply to the helping professions. He contended that journey metaphors are particularly useful because they connect people with powerful myths. The late Joseph Campbell (2008) discussed this at length in his various writings on the hero's journey. Certainly, there are many ways in which journey metaphors provide an apt way of describing the work of both clients and clinicians. Specific elements of a journey (searching for direction or needing a compass; not knowing which way to turn; feeling lost, broken down, or in foreign or unknown territory; wanting to take risks or experience new things but also maintain a feeling of security, and so forth) map onto social work intervention very closely. More important, Campbell's hero must go through struggles and hardships before attaining the status of a hero.

Metaphors across Bodies, Space, and Boundaries

Finally, social workers need to be aware of the important functional, living metaphors that may play an important ongoing role in clients' lives. An example of this is the relationship between one's body and the spaces one occupies, particularly one's home. People's body and home can be said to be the two most important containers in their lives, and they implicitly draw analogies from one to the other. Elderly people in particular may view the functional problems in their homes as experientially analogous to the physical problems they struggle with, especially when they have lived in their homes for many years and closely identify with them. Not only may the problems in their homes or property draw attention to their own ailments because they may have a decreased ability to attend to the former (for example, climb a ladder, fix carpentry or electrical problems, garden or mow, even use the stairs), but there may be specific home–body correlates that arise: The windows and doors creak as arthritis sets in; weeds sprout up more in the garden (or gutter) as hair grows in areas where it previously did not; the cracks in the paint become more noticeable as wrinkles spread on the face or body; the plumbing leaks more as incontinence looms, and so forth.

Spaces, including social service agencies and client homes and neighborhoods, can themselves be viewed metaphorically because they impart meaning to clients, workers, and the general public. The internal and external spatial components of social service agencies say something important about their mission and their perspective on those to whom they provide services. Dolmage (2011) wrote that "spaces and discourses work together to impose social order" (p. 55), and O'Donnell (2006) wrote that the "environment reflects, channels, facilitates, and shapes who communicates with whom, under what conditions, how, when, where, and in what context" (p. 214). O'Donnell added that architecture can be a symbol of ideology and that people "are often unaware of the persuasive and propagandistic effects that the environment has on them" (p. 221).

Metaphors are also frequently used, especially through mass media, to identify spaces and support demeaning stereotypes about particular communities or facilities that are occupied by marginalized populations (G. D. Adams & Cantor, 2001). Communities may be labeled as blighted if such a designation is helpful in having a neighborhood condemned for eminent domain purposes (Pinker, 2008; Wiley, 1990). Just as individuals or families may take on a stigmatized identity, so too may communities and, by association, those who live in them.

As I discuss further in chapter 2, metaphors are often embodied, or developed at a basic level, through people's personal and sensory experiences as they move through life (Gregg, 2004). Social workers in particular should be aware of the important role that spaces (including one's body) may play in the lives of the people with whom they work. The spaces people occupy, and especially the ones social workers have a hand in creating or changing (and that help create and change them), say something important about those people, as well as their values, identities, and goals. Beyond this, both constructed and natural spaces may have a very important metaphoric impact on how people come to view the world around them. Metaphoric embodiment likely plays a particularly important role in regard to people with physical disabilities or other physical features that are judged by others to be nonnormative (Linton, 2007).

Another important metaphoric theme that cuts across the various levels of social work intervention relates to boundaries. People frequently view the world in terms of lines, boundaries, crossings, and so forth. This is discussed, for example, in relation to enmeshed relationships or families, personal isolation, feelings of personal violation, questions of who has access to the family or social system, who the gatekeepers are, and what informal rules they follow. Ben-Amitay, Buchbinder, and Torin (2015), in their study of women who were sexually victimized and the metaphors they used, noted that boundary metaphors were important in these women's view of their trauma and its continued impact. It goes without saying that boundary metaphors are extremely important in community-based social work and include issues such as geographic and institutional areas and their meaning and boundary crossings (or lack thereof). As further noted in the chapter 4 discussion of dehumanization, both theorists and propagandists have often speculated over the course of time where the proper boundaries of humanity lie and what groups properly belong there (Ritvo, 1995).

METAPHORS AND SOCIAL WORK EDUCATION

Some authors have contended that metaphors may be a beneficial mode of teaching social work students, especially for content areas in which creative forms of education may be necessary. James Forte (2009) wrote that metaphors could be useful in teaching human behavior in the social environment content, and Leela Thomas (2007) noted that in instances in which social work students find it hard to grasp important concepts related to statistics through traditional teaching methods, metaphor may be useful (also see Bougher, 2012). This makes sense because, as noted earlier, one of the major reasons for the frequent use of metaphors is to present complex issues through concrete, experiential examples.

Being able to understand or deconstruct metaphors and other forms of rhetoric is also an important—I would argue essential—aspect of critical thinking (Murdach, 2006). If social workers cannot grasp the meaning behind terminology, descriptions, or images and do not understand their proper context, how can they truly engage in critical thought related to these terms or images? Words in particular form the building blocks of dialogue and engagement, in social work and elsewhere. To assume that words have the same meaning for everyone; that certain words do not carry particular baggage (at least for some people); or that humans do not know how to wield words to hurt, cajole, comfort, embarrass, compliment, or manipulate others is simply wrong. If one gives credence to the power of words, as social workers surely must, one needs to embrace metaphors and their importance in human interaction and self-awareness. Metaphors are "an important vehicle to understand . . . the nature of the helping relationship" (Weinberg, 2005, p. 2) and of human interactions of all kinds. The better social workers are able to interpret metaphors, the better they will understand clients, students, colleagues, the profession itself, and, as the central theme of this book points out, how to operate successfully in the political arena.

METAPHORS ABOUT SOCIAL WORK

Metaphors can also provide a fruitful means for students and professionals to share their feelings about field placements, personal or professional frustrations or accomplishments, or particular clientele. This is especially true in relation to what Weinberg (2005) referred to as "outlaw emotions," or feelings that individuals may not want to directly express because of their perception that these feelings clash with the hegemonic view of social work.

In her analysis of descriptions of young low-income mothers by student workers, Weinberg (2005) delineated several examples of animalistic comparisons made by students, for example, comparing mothers with baboons, porcupines, and other animals. She questioned whether such perceptions support a hierarchical view that justifies to students the power imbalance in the worker–client relationship. Although one might respond in a judgmental fashion to such views, they can be a starting point for instructive discussions of what specific metaphors represent.

John Sumarah (1989), too, contended that various metaphor themes characterize social workers' view of their clients. As he noted, "Metaphors influence the manner in which people think and feel about themselves and others and the way in which they act and react to one another" (p. 19). In a study of British social workers, Chris Beckett (2003) noted that they frequently used military metaphors in their descriptions of their jobs. Many of these workers felt as though they were constantly under siege, and the formal use of military rhetoric in their jobs may have, without their being aware of it, led to more colloquial or informal expressions (for example, being bombarded by clients) that aligned with the metaphor.

More important, these metaphors said much about how these workers viewed not only their jobs, but also their clients, supervisors, and agency.[7]

Regardless of the extent to which social workers stop to think about it, metaphors are all around them and have much to do with the activities of the profession and the way they perceive the world. Although social workers may instinctively comprehend the usefulness of metaphors, it is unlikely that they often take the time to purposefully deconstruct them or attempt to understand the role they play in either their professional lives or the world around them. As many practitioners have found, the embedded metaphoric images that social workers carry around with them, or that they consciously develop, can either help or hinder their development, and understanding these images can be a fruitful source of assessment and intervention.

---

[7]One might assume that various types of organizational structures or policies or staff–client or staff–supervisor relationships will affect the formation of meta-metaphors that are taken on by an agency. Although war metaphors might be expected in agencies with a heavy focus on working with veterans, for example, they might also easily develop and spread in any agency that deals with involuntary clientele, where workers have to battle to gain client support, and obstinate clients could even be viewed as enemies in the context of the treatment process.

2
Metaphors and Denigration: Social Justice Implications

Semantic warfare . . . does not ordinarily burst upon the scene helter-skelter. It is not an accidental, spontaneous, or chaotic episode, but a deliberate and unremitting phenomenon usually undergirded by fully elaborated systems of concepts, beliefs, and myths.
—Brennan (1995, p. 12)

Whether people are seen as devils or monsters, germs or vermin, pigs or apes, as robots, or as abstract menaces, they are thus removed from the company of men and exposed to the defenses we employ against those threats.
—Sanford and Comstock (1971, p. 7)

As alluded to in the preceding chapter, in addition to providing a general frame for how a target group or issue is described, conceptual metaphors "can influence the way information [about the target] is processed and represented in memory" (Allbritton, 1995, p. 38). Additional knowledge about the person, group, event, or issue that one confronts after making a metaphoric connection is considered in the light of this pre-existing relationship. Such information or examples may be interpreted in a specific way on the basis of their perceived relevance and how well such information maps onto the metaphor.

In other words, people seek out information sources that support their preferred framings, and once a particular conceptual metaphor is widely embraced as an apt way of viewing the target, it may be extremely difficult to replace it with a contrasting mode of framing. This is particularly true in cases in which the existing frame closely relates to emotional feelings such as disgust, fear, or anger (De Vos & Suárez-Orozco, 1990). Indeed, a major contention of this book is that although social workers and other allies for social justice should strive to destigmatize various groups or conditions, it is very difficult to do so once a particular demeaning image has been formed, disseminated, and widely embraced. Framings, or "schemas," to use Winter's (2008) term, are a central element in stereotyping and stigmatization. Metaphors serve as "economic vehicles to communicate stereotypes because they provide an efficient synthesis of the most relevant characteristics" (Maass, Suitner, & Arcuri, 2014, p. 164).

DISGUST, FEAR, AND LOATHING

To expand on this thought, disgust, fear, loathing, and related emotions are particularly important metaphoric vehicles because they largely affect people on a subconscious level (Chapman & Anderson, 2013; Charteris-Black, 2011). Fear especially is considered to be a very primitive emotion, and it often operates in ways people neither understand nor fully appreciate (Nussbaum, 2004). Disgust reactions are closely tied to contamination concerns and people's basic need to protect their bodily integrity from perceived threats from the outside environment, including other people (Beck, 2011; O'Brien, 2018; Rozin, Haidt, & McCauley, 2009). Disability scholars, for example, have noted that fear and apprehension of people with disabilities closely relates to this inherent need to protect oneself and one's loved ones from contagion, even if one realizes on a logical level that disabilities are not communicable (Livneh, 1991). Even years after HIV was known to only be transmissible through direct blood-to-blood contact, people remained wary of the possibility of any form of contact with people who were so diagnosed, even when they knew actual contagion was a virtual impossibility (Rozin, Markwith, & McCauley, 1994). Public health initiatives of all types must often take into account the discomforting fact that risk avoidance is as much (if not more) related to inherent responses than to the actual possibility of harm (Glassner, 1999). Donileen Loseke (2003) was certainly correct in writing that "it is not possible to argue that Americans worry about what we should worry about" (pp. 9–10; also see Glassner, 1999).

In the following chapters, I return to this theme, describing the importance of not only such emotions but how they have been used, often purposefully exploited, as a rhetorical vehicle to diminish respect for various devalued groups. Many of the examples that I provide in chapters 4 and 5 not only have relevance in the way in which various subpopulations and social problems are viewed but also, as noted earlier, have an impact on the social work profession itself and the sanction social workers are accorded to render specific services. Sanction for the activities of social workers and other licensed professionals is not purely an academic concern, especially at a time when an increasing number of job areas are being given over to nonprofessionals and when economic factors such as profit making and cost cutting are often core institutional values.

The profession needs to be aware of how dehumanizing metaphoric themes are used not only to denigrate vulnerable populations, but also to devalue social work itself. The public relations aspect of social work relates not just to social workers' professional ego, it also has great importance in how (and whether) agencies are funded and supported by public, private, and political stakeholders. Programs and services that are largely perceived as useless or as promoting dependency or negative social values are vulnerable, especially during times of economic hardship (Abromovitz, 2005). In this chapter, I further explore this topic and lay the groundwork for chapters 4 and 5 by introducing the role of pejorative metaphor themes in denigrating already vulnerable groups. First, however, it is important to explore how metaphors work conceptually and their important impact on the decisions people make in their day-to-day lives.

METAPHORS AND HOW PEOPLE THINK

Recent scholarship has shed important light on the fact that specific metaphors do influence how people think about events, issues, and groups. Much of this "recent work . . . has suggested that these metaphors are more than simply colorful ways of talking. Using different metaphors leads people to reason differently about social issues and follow different paths of inference" (Thibodeau, Iyiewaure, & Boroditsky, 2015, p. 2374). Hauser and Schwarz (2015), for example, conducted a study in which a group of participants was primed to view cancer as an enemy, using the war metaphor that is frequently attached to the disease. As in similar studies that have been conducted along these lines, the primes[1] were very subtle and usually went unnoticed by participants. The group members

---

[1] "Priming" is described as the use of terms, phrases, or even images that relate, often covertly, to a particular metaphor to elicit responses that are in keeping with the metaphoric theme. In this section, I provide examples of such priming.

who were exposed to this framing, as opposed to the control group, whose framing was neutral, were more apt to support forms of prevention that operated in conjunction with the metaphor. The authors contended that those who were subject to the war framing were less likely to consider those forms of prevention that did not coexist well with the war metaphor, such as self-limitation behaviors (for example, not smoking, limiting salt) (Hauser & Schwarz, 2015; also see Reisfeld & Wilson, 2004).

Fear and Loathing Responses

In similar studies, Thibodeau and Boroditsky (2011) demonstrated that the crime prevention activities that subjects were likely to support were affected by subtle metaphors that described crime as a virus (which leads to support for community prevention and education programs) or as a beast (which lends itself to support for imprisonment and other law enforcement responses).

Probably the most prevalent example of how funding and service streams are affected by a specific frame is the use of the war metaphor in relation to drug funding. As is frequently discussed, the War on Drugs framing serves to direct funding to harsh modes of prevention such as law enforcement and imprisonment, whereas the use of disease or health framings for illegal drug use would more likely result in resources being devoted to treatment and education (Ellwood, 1995; also see Burke, 1992).[2] Dodge (2008) noted that differential framing of juvenile violence can affect where funding for related programs is directed, and Barry, Brescoll, Brownell, and Schlesinger (2009) noted that how obesity is framed can affect where blame for the problem is placed (individual, food industry, society at large) and therefore what specific public policies (and thus funding streams) are supported relative to the issue.

Disgust Responses

To revisit an important theme, some of the more interesting research related to the impact metaphors have on personal decision making has related to disgust or contagion responses, which are closely correlated with each other and are directly connected to the groups and problems that many social workers deal with. Landau, Sullivan, and Greenberg

---

[2]One might contend that people indeed do infuse disease metaphors into drug discussions, but these metaphors are directed more at addiction among more respected groups in society, who are framed as victims (addicts) rather than as criminals.

(2009) tested the hypothesis that people's need to protect their bodies from potential contagion would affect the feelings subjects had regarding undocumented immigrants, under the assumption that fears of intrusion of outside entities into one's physical body would subconsciously lead subjects to be concerned about intrusion of foreign bodies into the country. The researchers primed subjects in the experimental group by having them read an article on the threat of airborne bacteria, and all subjects were then asked questions related to immigration. Although the article did not make a direct connection between bacteria and immigration, the subjects who were primed with the bacteria article expressed greater threat of illegal immigration than those who were not so primed. Landau et al. noted that "induced motivation to protect the literal body interacted with a body-metaphoric framing of the United States, resulting in more negative reactions toward U.S. immigration" (p. 1426; also see O'Brien, 2003a, 2018).

As this example demonstrates, and as introduced in the preceding chapter, many metaphors that have particular salience for humans are those that relate to embodiment, those sensory or physical phenomena that people have personally experienced (Bougher, 2012). Among others, Geary (2012), Lee and Schwartz (2013), Risen and Critcher (2011), and Zhong and House (2013) have provided copious examples of psychological studies that relate to embodiment: People who are made to use antiseptic wipes or wash their hands may feel less sinful (more cleansed) than those who do not, people are more likely to judge an issue as important or weighty when they are holding a heavy object, individuals in warmer rooms are apt to judge global warming to be an issue of greater concern than those in colder rooms, and so forth. As Geary has written, "Our bodies prime our metaphors, and our metaphors prime how we think and act" (p. 100).

As the authors cited in this section acknowledge, the role that metaphor primes play in people's decision making is quite complex. The impact of such metaphors depends on an interconnected set of issues that include, among other factors, the perceived relationship between source and target domains and an individual's pre-existing views on the topic at hand. People are much more likely to be affected by primes in relation to issues that they have not thought much about or taken firm positions on. Nonetheless, the evidence demonstrates that metaphors can not only affect people's decision making related to social issues and groups, but do so in ways that normally go unnoticed.

Metaphor Priming, Prejudice, and Bias

It is important to note that these and other studies on priming are not only relevant to social welfare policy solutions, but they are also a jumping-off point for understanding implicit or underlying prejudice or bias. Moreover, they may also provide a key to understanding how such bias occurs and the degree to which it subconsciously affects one's own decision making (Hall et al., 2015). Nicolas and Skinner (2012) conducted a study that included priming experimental subjects with the term "gay," used in a derogatory way in the course of a written dialogue between two people. Those subjects so primed had more negative attitudes toward gays and lesbians on the Implicit Association Test, a scale frequently used to measure implicit bias, than did subjects who were given alternative terms, such as "lame." Boysen (2009) wrote that "counseling research should reflect the changing perspectives on bias with an increased focus on subtle, unintentional bias" (p. 240). Awareness of metaphor priming research can also inform clinical practice, perhaps providing useful information that can have an impact on both assessment and treatment.

METAPHORS AND THE FRAMING OF MARGINALIZED GROUPS

As many scholars (for example, Brennan, 1995; Keen, 1986; O'Brien, 2013, 2018; D. L. Smith, 2011; Wolfensberger, 1972) have noted, a select pool of pejorative metaphoric themes have been used over time for the purpose of denigrating different marginalized community groups, and the way these themes "transcend time, distance and culture is remarkable" (Wolfensberger, 1972, p. 16).[3] In *Worse than War*, his book on genocidal actions, Daniel Goldhagen (2009) contended,

> How does this [genocide] come about? Not through peer pressure, not through blind obedience to authority, not because modernity has transformed people into bureaucrats, and not due to any other reductionist notion that has been posited in defiance of the historical record. It comes about through language and visual images as the bearers of cultural notions,

---
[3] A version of some of the content in this section was previously published in O'Brien (2009).

Metaphors and Denigration 31

> including how to understand humanity and, in particular, other disparaged peoples and groups. . . . Language is the primary medium for preparing people to support or perpetrate mass murder and elimination, because it is the vehicle for conceptualizing, conveying, and making persuasive the necessary prejudices and ideas. (p. 311)

The denigration that supports oppressive actions of all types is maintained by a "stable, patterned set of beliefs, tropes, symbols and charges" (p. 313) that cut across dehumanizing cultures and periods.

In some cases, metaphor themes may be transmitted virtually whole cloth from one out-group to another. An example of this is the movement, especially prevalent in the 1970s and 1980s, to frame gay men as a "shadow in the land" (Dannemeyer, 1989). This presentation of gay men as a secretive, powerful, conspiratorial, amoral group that is intent on corrupting youths and bringing down Christian America bears a striking resemblance to the metaphoric representation of Communist sympathizers during the McCarthy era. Certainly the 1950s image of people who were purported in sensitive government posts to be closeted (and easily blackmailed) gay men fostered this connection (McCarthy, 1952), along with the fact that many of the individuals and groups who were responsible for developing the former image were involved in framing the early anti–gay rights agenda. The use of previous pejorative tropes may allow oppressors to draw on previously established control infrastructures and networks, in addition to providing a ready-made denigrating image of the target group with which the public is already familiar.

Power Relationships

These modes of viewing issues and groups obviously involve power relationships, because those with power (and the means to widely disseminate their views, often through the control of media platforms) seek to identify and define those with little power in a way that promotes their own interests. To quote Yoosun Park (2008b), a social work professor at Smith College of Social Work,

> Language and discourse are viewed not as impartial tools which describe reality, but as constitutive modes of power that construct unequal identities with differential material consequences, privileging some as legitimate and normative and

> rendering others, by the rules of these privileged constructions, as de-legitimized and non-normative. (p. 773)

As Park (2008b) noted in this work as well as in others (Park, 2008a; Park & Kemp, 2006), social workers have in the past been influenced by and frequently used the same derogatory rhetoric and stereotypic views that have been in vogue in the general population. This negative framing provides some explanation for why the profession, which has ordinarily embraced the notion of social justice, has itself engaged in various forms of oppression over the years, such as immigration restriction, supporting the administrative infrastructure for Japanese internment (Park, 2008a), the identification or restriction of immigrants and refugees (Moran & Gillett, 2014; Park, 2008b), racial segregation, eugenic policies such as involuntary sterilization and segregation (LaPan & Platt, 2005; O'Brien, 1999, 2013), and other adverse actions.

Social Control

As a general rule, advocating for social control measures against vulnerable populations does not sit well with the belief that one is supportive of social justice, and even those who engage in the most oppressive forms of control do not want to be perceived as acting inhumanely or without compelling justification. Whenever, therefore, widespread efforts are made to control, disparage, or even exterminate stigmatized people, various rationales are used to portray the target group as a threat to society, a subhuman entity, or both. Even Hitler couched his anti-Semitic and other programs in the rhetoric of self-defense: Jews, homosexuals, Gypsies, people with contagious diseases, socialists, and others were all corruptive social entities who had the ability to bring down the nation if strong action was not taken (Proctor, 1988). Joseph Goebbels, Hitler's closest adviser, wrote the following, which appeared in a major U.S. publication the year before Hitler gained the chancellorship:

> Of course the Jew is a human being. No one of us has ever doubted that. But so is the flea a kind of animal, though not a very pleasant one. And, since the flea is not a pleasant kind of animal, is it not our conscientious duty to protect ourselves against him and to kill him when he bites and annoys us so that he will not do us harm? The Jews should be treated in the same way. (Goebbels, 1932, p. 391)

Metaphors and Denigration

Those who support a program of control will often also rely on altruistic rationales as a means of psychologically justifying their position. They present themselves as acting not only for the betterment of society, but also for the victims themselves. As I further discuss in chapter 4, even the most egregious human rights violations are likely to include altruistic rationales. Slaveholders, for example, argued that slaves would not survive if freed, and it is often contended that infants with severe disabilities should be left to die because allowing them to live with a disability is a cruelty. Altruistic rationales frame oppressors as supportive of those who are oppressed and as acting in their best interests.

Efforts to enforce formal social control policies are especially prevalent in the context of alarm periods, which are characterized by a passionate display of anger, fear, or both regarding the potential negative and even destructive societal impact of target groups. These periods are marked by public policy proposals to restrict the rights of target group members, such as by removing them from the community through their placement into asylums, ghettos, work or internment camps, prisons, or similar segregated environments; deporting them from the nation altogether; reducing their freedom to assemble, speak, or procreate; increasing government surveillance of their activities; or, in the case of the most flagrant alarm periods, killing them outright. In such cases, the employment of dehumanizing or threat-inducing rhetoric is particularly necessary because such actions normally run counter to important cultural beliefs, such as the acceptance of diversity, equal treatment, constitutionally based freedoms, and the right to due process. As Levin (1971) contended, a principal attribute of alarm movements, and the rhetoric that fuels them, is that they "excite deep unconscious wishes and anxieties and tap primitive and infantile ways of thinking" (p. 144). Alarm periods may also produce a vehicle, in the form of the targeted out-group, onto which free-floating anxieties are displaced. During times of high anxiety, people look for a tangible source of this anxiety, and various individuals, groups, and organizations that have a stake in oppressive policies will compete with one another to have their targets accepted as a principal source of fear. De Landtsheer (1994) contended that in times of public anxiety, such as an economic recession, metaphoric language is more predominant in political discussions.

Metaphors and Stereotyping

As I discuss further in the next chapter, the use of metaphors to foster a pejorative image of the target group also objectifies those who presumably belong to the group by stereotyping them and casting all members into the same "worst-case" condition. If those accused of sexual molestation are all monsters, recipients of Temporary Assistance to Needy Families are all parasites, and people with severe disabilities are all vegetables, one need not attend to the uniqueness of each case but can simply view the class as a whole and develop restrictive policies that most clearly fit the prevailing stereotype (Lens, 2005). Reinarman and Levine (1995) described the term "routinization of caricature," whereby "worst cases [are] framed as typical cases" (p. 160).

Moreover, once a denigrating label sticks and policies are developed to control its members, the net can be widened to bring in a more expansive group of devalued people. A diagnostic and control infrastructure develops and expands, and professional groups associated with this infrastructure need to justify its existence and promote its growth (Gergen, 1999). In fact, at times various conditions or diagnoses may fall under the weight of this large mass of potential subjects who are brought under such control. Once the term "moron" was created in 1910 as a way of designating the highest functioning class of feebleminded people and IQ tests were developed to identify who rightly belonged in this group, an ever-increasing percentage of the population came to be so identified, until it was patently obvious that the condition was much too vague and expansive (Gould, 1981; O'Brien & Bundy, 2009). The closer a designation comes to affecting those whom people consider to be like them, the more it will come under scrutiny.

Concern about an issue will also likely diminish after the development of a diagnostic and control infrastructure because such an infrastructure was a principal goal of advocates all along (Reinarman & Levine, 1995). Once this goal is reached, the issue does not have to stay in the news. By the time the fear brought forth by eugenicists waned in the 1920s, mass IQ testing and involuntary sterilization and institutionalization practices had become formalized.

The combining of negative identities further ensures that people can be maintained on the outside margins of society (Metzl, 2009). Over time, there have been continued attempts, for example, to connect designations

Metaphors and Denigration

of physical or mental disability to women, people of color, immigrants, and other devalued populations. Dolmage (2011) wrote that during the immigration restriction era of the early 1900s, designations such as "feebleminded" and "psychopathic inferiority" were so vague that they "allowed any noticeably foreign body to be made inferior" (p. 47). Questions related to a person's racial heritage or identification have also served to prove a differing marginal status, as when miscegenation within a family was used to confirm feeblemindedness in eugenic family studies (Rafter, 1988).

To properly identify which deviant or devalued subgroups are to be denigrated through word- or image-based metaphors, some system of classification and surveillance needs to be developed. In his classic book *Stigma* (Goffman, 1963), as well as in many of his other writings (Goffman, 1959, 1961), Erving Goffman discussed at length the need to classify or stigmatize such individuals to position them on the margins of society. He also described efforts by people who could be so identified or diagnosed to pass as nonstigmatized. Metaphors serve to enhance diagnostic representation and advance the notion that what may in reality be socially constructed categories do indeed make logical sense and that they have a basis in science, objectivity, or some form of professional expertise.

In many cases in which a particular stigma status is unclear, people are often required to self-identify. The Jim Crow laws and rules of etiquette that were in place in many Southern communities, for example, were one way that people of mixed race or others with uncertain heritage were required to identify which race they belonged to.[4] Those who attempted to pass as white were obviously subject to very harsh treatment if found out, in part because their liminal status pointed to the fact that such boundary drawing was indeed based on social and political rather than natural or scientific definitions (Gross, 2010). To quote René Girard (1989), "Despite what is said around us persecutors are never obsessed by difference but rather by its unutterable contrary, the lack of difference" (p. 22).

---

[4] As Grace Hale (1998) wrote in *Making Whiteness,* even when businesses served both white and African American customers, rules of etiquette were in place (for example, allowing white customers to move ahead in line) to not only oppress African Americans, but also require them to self-identify. These rules obviously became more important as mobility increased throughout the nation (for example, the Great Migration of African Americans that began around 1916), because newcomers' family history (and therefore their racial classification) was often unknown. In spaces marked by both a large heterogeneous population and frequent migration, such as New York City, a thriving line of businesses developed (for example, hair straightening and facial bleaching) to allow African Americans or those of mixed ancestry to pass as white, often so they could obtain a job or live in a white area of the city. Also see Gross's (2010) *What Blood Won't Tell.*

The metaphors that are used to disparage marginalized groups therefore also serve to provide a master status, or central identifying feature, for those who belong to these groups. This master status is imposed on them by the majority to set them off from the norm and place them firmly within the boundaries of the devalued group. As noted previously, various social norms are developed to ensure that those who are so identified remain objectified. How the use of these denigrating metaphor themes interrelates with identity, the marking of individuals as stigmatized, and continued surveillance and control efforts, and a number of examples of this, are included in the following chapters.

METAPHORS AND THE PUBLIC IMAGE OF SOCIAL WORK

To adequately provide competent services, social workers and other allies for social justice need to be concerned about not only their image but moreover their credibility, especially because assumptions about this credibility will have an impact on funding and service delivery.[5] Just as those with whom they work are frequently stereotyped, so too are social workers, and enhancing their perceived credibility relates to the ability to understand the negative metaphoric images that the public often has of the profession. Social workers must understand how these stereotypes formed and who gains from them because these stereotypes are not just out there, arising organically from the ether; they are politically and economically useful to certain constituencies who will fight efforts to change them. Professionals need to be capable of deconstructing these images of the profession and effectively countering them.

Social workers would generally attest to the fact that many people with whom they come into contact, even people they know well, have only a cursory awareness of the populations with whom or social problems with which they work. Many social workers know too well the freezing effect their profession carries with it. At a gathering or party, or simply when meeting someone new, the response to the query "So what do you do?" often freezes the conversation or forces it to turn uncomfortably in a different direction. Other than the standard back-handed compliments ("Oh, you must have a lot of patience"; "That must be so rewarding";

---

[5] A version of some of the content in this section was previously published in O'Brien (2009).

"I've got to hand it to you, I could never do what you do"), most people generally would prefer not to discuss exactly what it is social workers do or with whom they do it.

Stigmas in Social Work

To some degree, social workers understand that the adverse reaction just described is due to the courtesy stigma that is attached to social work (Goffman, 1963). Because many of those with whom social workers work (welfare recipients, sexual offenders, parents who have been accused of abuse or neglect, those who have committed violent felonies, individuals with chronic mental illness, and so forth) are considered among the most undesirable groups in society, the adverse reaction to these groups is through association attached to social workers.[6] To pick up on the train of thought shared earlier, social workers' experiences with marked people and working in what are presumed to be despoiled surroundings contaminate and taint them and also threaten to taint those with whom they come into contact. W. I. Miller (1997) wrote that "when something disgusts us ... we feel tainted, burdened by the belief that anything that comes into contact with the disgusting thing also acquires the capacity to disgust as a consequence of that contact" (p. 12).

Although I may be accused of hyperbole here, many scholars have written extensively about the subliminal power of disgust and contagion reactions (Beck, 2011; Douglas, 1984), and empirical evidence in support of the powerful impact of what one might refer to as psychological contagion is growing (Chapman & Anderson, 2013; Rozin et al., 2009). I revisit the issue in chapter 5 and discuss in greater depth why disgust and contagion play such an important role in the pantheon of public fear, as well as its direct relevance to the social work profession.

As noted, awareness of metaphor use can help one more fully understand how the profession is viewed by others. Consider the following quote, which appeared in a 1993 *National Review* article on the topic of welfare reform:

---

[6] In her various writings, Candice Clark (1987, 1998) discussed sympathy giving and the etiquette that surrounds sympathy. Her research may provide additional insight into why social workers and other allies for social justice are often viewed in a negative light. As she noted, culture dictates that there is an appropriate amount of sympathy that is to be provided for specific types of situations. When sympathy givers go beyond this, as many presume social workers do on a regular basis, they are perceived as providing an undue amount of sympathy to those who deserve little.

> Work requirements are catnip for social workers; they see counseling galore in the educational programs and training seminars that Congress will construe as meeting the requirements. Result: A new sandbox for the welfare bureaucracies to romp in. Social workers sometimes grumble about work requirements, for the sake of appearances; secretly they love them. (Bethell, 1993, p. 34)

This selection provides a particularly good example of the use of metaphors for the purpose of supporting entrenched pejorative stereotypes related to the profession. The disquiet or even anger that social workers might feel in reading this selection probably goes beyond simply their visceral response to the dehumanizing metaphors, in which social workers are animalized (as cats) and infantilized (as playing in sandboxes). Indeed, such representations carry a depth of meaning that is difficult to fully ascertain except on close analysis. The assumed selfish intent of social workers—who are said to be motivated simply by their base physical urges, as are animals and children—that permeates the quote is reinforced by both metaphors. Moreover, additional meaning can be applied to the cat metaphor, because cats are generally viewed as feminine animals, and the social work profession is largely composed of women. Also, as an aside, one knows what cats like to do in sandboxes. Objectifying a vast range of professionals as members of the welfare bureaucracies similarly serves to cast the entire profession in an adverse light. Finally, social workers are presented as inherently dishonest, complaining about something they secretly want because it provides job security.

Social workers are presented here as self-centered people who are looking for ways to take advantage of a bloated and ineffectual bureaucratic system to serve their own ends, exploiting both clients and taxpayers along the way. For many social workers who are overworked, overwhelmed, underpaid, and fighting burnout, the use of the simple term "romp" may be enough to put them over the proverbial edge. Among the many things that social workers do, they decidedly do not romp. The term minimizes and demeans the practice of social work in a way that few other simple terms could match. In effect, one does not have to look too far to see that this short selection includes much of the negative representational baggage that the profession carries, at least in the eyes of many. Like their clients, social workers are presented here as parasites, taking hard-earned tax money, fostering dependency, and providing little of use in return.

Reframing the Public Image of Social Work

Inappropriate, hurtful, or disturbing comments related to the profession can often be seen in social media and other public forums, and social workers must be forceful in countering these images, or at least develop a very thick skin. In August 2015, a Vermont social worker was killed by a client after the client's child was removed from the home. Although one might think that a situation such as this one would call for compassion and thoughts and prayers for the family of the deceased, the comment section of one social media site that carried the article (Yahoo News) was awash in diatribes about invasive child protective agencies ruining families' lives. Many comments began "Although I don't condone violence" or "Nothing justifies murder, but. . . ." An assessment of just a few dozen of these comments showed that social workers were referred to as "strangers" or "kidnappers" (multiple appearances) who "come into our homes and dictate our lives"; "invaders" with "Gestapo-like power" who "mess with people's children," "manufacture" claims and evidence, and use a "scorched earth policy." One commenter noted that although he did not "know about this specific case . . . I can certainly understand and even validate that there are several caseworkers that need to be shot in order to save kids." An important issue to note in relation to this case was that the article provided virtually no specific information about why the child was removed from the home (Associated Press, 2015). These horrendous comments were fully based on readers' assumptions rather than any factual knowledge of this particular case.

As noted previously, because areas such as child welfare, and especially abuse investigations or outplacement, are highly emotionally charged, logic and the provision of supporting rationales may play a role in the profession's response to negative public perceptions, but it is likely to be more beneficial to find alternative means of framing or different metaphoric descriptors because logic itself is unlikely to cause people to question the existing narrative. It is very hard if not impossible to overcome high emotion through rational counterarguments, especially with respect to deep-set sociopolitical issues.

When social work organizations engage in public relations efforts, it is important that they take into account the metaphors that are used and consider how these metaphors are generally interpreted. Such efforts should also consider the implicit or underlying views (positive or negative) others have of the profession and the relationship of these messages to emotional responses to the profession.

It is crucial that social workers understand the nature of pejorative metaphor themes and images if they are to advocate effectively for their clients. In many cases, this means gaining an awareness of the historical precursors of such metaphors as well as how they work on a subconscious emotional level. Knowledge of diversity and social justice issues will be enhanced by comprehending these adverse themes and how the historical weight of this form of denigration continues to place vulnerable groups in defensive positions. Especially in cases in which new target groups are singled out and stigmatized images have not been fully embraced or carried over to such groups, social workers need to be actively engaged in countering such images and ensuring that they are not used to undergird policies of control and restriction.

3
Metaphors and Social Welfare Policy

> *Because so much of our social and political reasoning makes use of this system of metaphorical concepts, any adequate appreciation of even the most mundane social and political thought requires an understanding of this system.*
> —Lakoff (1995, p. 177)
>
> *Shifts in metaphors are often accompanied by shifts in policy.*
> —Thibodeau and Boroditsky (2011, p. 1)

Through introductory philosophy or critical thinking classes, many social workers have become familiar, perhaps begrudgingly so, with syllogisms. A syllogism may be a helpful way of putting forth the important thesis of this book, and so I begin with the following:

> Statement A: Virtually all social work practice is fundamentally based on social policy.
>
> Statement B: A central element of social policy is the use of metaphor themes to support various policy options.

Therefore,

> all social work practice is heavily influenced by the use of specific policy-related metaphor themes. The short version may be stated thus: "If social work practice (A) is heavily influenced by policy (B), and policy (B) is heavily influenced by metaphors (C), then social work practice (A) is heavily influenced by policy-related metaphors (C)."

One may question either the veracity of one or both of these particular statements or the connection provided between the two. In this chapter, I provide arguments in support of both the particular statements themselves and their conjoining. I first consider the importance of policy for the social work field, focusing on practice within the profession, the impact of policies on agency service delivery options, and the training of students in social work education programs vis-à-vis client advocacy. I next discuss the extensive use of metaphors in the context of social policy analysis. These metaphors provide a means of viewing societal subgroups or social problems through a preferred lens or framing. These framings support specific policy options over competing ways of viewing the group or issue, which further serves to increase or decrease, sometimes dramatically, the amount of funding provided to respond to an issue or diverts funding specifically to agencies, programs, or industrial sectors that best match the desired framing. I note up front that neither of the statements I have put forth is original or very controversial. As I further describe, the first has been discussed extensively by social work academics and policy advocates for decades and the second has been subject to extensive research by rhetoricians and political analysts. What is somewhat novel is joining the two together.

POLICY–PRACTICE CONNECTION IN SOCIAL WORK

The major way in which social policy forms the foundation for social work practice is that virtually all social welfare agencies benefit, directly or indirectly, from government funding and related policy decisions that affect their ability to offer specific services to a particular clientele. Such funding is often essential to the development and continued operation of an agency. Agencies frequently contract with federal, state, county, or local authorities to provide specific services and are in turn required to abide by the requirements set forth by these authorities. Governmental units may institute very specific guidelines, which will have an impact on the type of services that may be provided by the agency, clientele served, staffing issues such as credentialing and staff–client ratios, and a broad range of additional treatment-related elements.[1]

---

[1] It is important to add that such limitations have expanded with the continued focus on managed care and other efforts at cost cutting, especially in the range of treatments that are allowed for

The policy elements that specifically pertain to social work and related professions are layered on top of the broad policies that affect employers in general, such as safety and health regulations (for example, Occupational Safety and Health Administration policies), employee benefit and leave policies, antidiscrimination requirements, and community zoning regulations. As Leon Ginsberg (1996) wrote,

> Little happens in the human services unless there is social policy to authorize, sanction and pay for it. So . . . the practice of the human services professions is a product of social policy, and social policy is fundamental to everything else that goes on in human services work. (p. 6)

Government funding and therefore tax dollars are the lifeblood of many, if not most, social service agencies, and the health of any particular agency may rise or fall in large part on the basis of the vagaries of the political system, changes in the economy or public feelings about taxes, or media coverage of cases that draw public attention to specific social problems and serve as framing incidents. Martin Rein (1971) was prescient when he wrote almost half a century ago that "institutional arrangements themselves imply ideological meaning" (p. 301).

Case for Social Worker Involvement

The involvement of social workers in the policy arena and the inclusion of policy practice content in social work education is emphasized in large part because of the need for professional advocacy not only in support of one's own agency, but also for the overall provision of services to a population or a national or global response to a public need (Jansson, 2001). If social workers do not advocate on behalf of agencies and clients, these services become vulnerable. As noted previously, social workers often feel uncomfortable operating in the policy arena and want to leave it to others who have more expertise or comfort in the area. These others, however, will often be politicians and other stakeholders who have little knowledge of or interest in social work clientele or the profession. They may operate from a conceptual starting point that draws heavily on stereotypes and misconceptions, and they may invoke derogatory metaphors as a guide for judging the usefulness of social services to particular groups. To put

---

treatment of people diagnosed with mental illness.

social workers' jobs, their clients' welfare, and agencies' viability in their hands is beyond foolish.[2]

Too frequently, social work professionals only understand the importance of policy practice when their jobs or agencies are in dire jeopardy, although learning to lobby effectively at the last minute is certainly not a recipe for success. Especially in tough economic times, such as a recession, social service funding may be one of the first areas to be cut. Social work clients are unfortunately neither highly valued by many nor do they have the resources to engage in public relations efforts to diminish the pervasive stereotypes that foster this devaluation. Social workers need to develop ongoing relationships with legislators and other political stakeholders and should be the principal educators of legislators when it comes to social service issues.[3]

The inclusion of policy awareness and advocacy in the Ethical Standards of the *Code of Ethics of the National Association of Social Workers* (NASW) acknowledges the important connection between policy and competent practice. Among its other policy-related statements, the code states that "social workers should be aware of the impact of the political arena on practice and should advocate for changes in policy and legislation to improve social conditions to meet basic human needs and promote social justice" (NASW, 2017, section 6.04). Policy advocacy is also included as one of the nine competencies set forth by the Council on Social Work Education (2015) for both BSW and MSW training of social work students. An argument can be made that this is among the most important of those competencies because the others all derive from policy. Human rights and diversity are obviously closely tied to policy engagement, but it does not take much thought to realize the various ways

---

[2] For 15 or so years, I have supervised BSW students at our department's annual lobby day activities in Springfield, Illinois. In the context of this project, I have often been taken aback by how surprised students are when they discover that certain legislators display little understanding of the particular social service issue students are focusing on or that these individuals, who make crucial social welfare decisions and direct millions of dollars, may share the same inaccurate negative stereotypes—about populations in need, service delivery, or the nature of the social work profession—under which members of the general public often operate.

[3] The employees of nonprofit agencies do, however, have to understand the limitations that are placed on their acting as lobbyists. Generally, they are limited by law in using government funding to directly lobby, especially for particular legislation or politicians. However, the belief that employees of nonprofits are completely unable to lobby, especially with respect to policies that have a direct impact on their agencies, is not accurate. Especially as private citizens, social workers have the same rights to advocate as do all citizens.

in which effective social work practice and thus the additional competencies are directly affected by policy development.

As noted earlier, beyond social services funding, policies directly affect marginalized populations in a host of ways, including nondiscrimination legislation and human rights protection. If social workers accept their role as advocates for human rights and diversity, it is difficult to see how this would be practiced outside of the policy arena. As macro-level social work scholars have frequently pointed out, although advocacy for a particular client, family, or neighborhood is certainly important, advocacy on a more expansive community, interest group, or even international level may benefit many individuals with similar issues and also serve to help prevent problems from occurring in the future for others who are at risk. To use an interesting policy metaphor that has recently gained traction, working on human rights and economic justice on a case-by-case basis is much like playing an unending game of whack-a-mole.

Dorothea Dix: Her Impact on Policy Practice in Social Work

This emphasis on the policy arena has a long history in social welfare advocacy. A half century before the profession of social work even existed, Dorothea Dix spent a great deal of time and effort courting legislators and attempting to support the passage of policies she felt would benefit populations in need. In the decades before the Civil War, Dix journeyed throughout various states and assessed the way in which people with mental illness were treated. After compiling information on numerous cases of inhumane treatment or outright neglect, Dix spent long hours cajoling legislators and attempting to convince taxpayers of their duty to support her efforts. She argued that preventive care was particularly beneficial, stating that "humanity and economy are both largely concerned in the prompt and judicious treatment of the insane in the first stages of the disease" ("Memorial of Miss Dix," 1863, p. 13). A particularly important event in the nation's history of social welfare was when Dix's major attempt to gain federal support for the development of institutions was stymied by a veto by then-President Franklin Pierce, who argued that care for those in need was a state or local rather than a federal concern. "Begin with doing anything for the indigent insane," he noted, "and soon will the federal government have on its hands the support of every sick man, every vagabond, every drunkard, in the land!"

(cited in Tiffany, 1891, pp. 199–200). Unfortunately, Pierce's philosophy carries wide support to this day.[4]

Although the veto of her proposal was very difficult for Dix to accept, her efforts in the state legislatures were generally much more successful (Lindhorst, 2002). Certainly, the massive mental institutions that were developed in the decades after Dix's time have come to be seen as the epitome of benign neglect and bureaucracy run amok. It should be noted, however, that the facilities she envisioned were much smaller and would have provided humane treatment, or at least what would have passed for humane treatment at the time.[5] Part of the Dorothea Dix story, then, is the importance of persistent political advocacy efforts over time and the development of an advocacy infrastructure that can ensure continued monitoring and evaluation of political gains. I would argue that an important feature of this infrastructure needs to be the ongoing appraisal of derogatory images and terminology that are used to devalue groups and thus support limitations on their basic rights or access to services.[6]

Dorothea Dix's influence was important to the many advocates who would follow in her wake. Very few important human rights or social justice policies have been passed because legislators have seen the light and simply decided to do the right thing. In virtually all cases, such policies are signed into law because of relentless pressure from professional and client or family advocacy groups or the confluence of political, social, and economic factors that force politicians' hand. In those cases in which legislators themselves have played an integral role in pushing such legislation, it has often been because they or their family have been directly affected by the issue at hand.[7] Policy analyst John Kingdon (2003) used

---

[4] As an interesting aside, Dix frequently used metaphors in her own writings, in particular describing in graphic detail the animalistic treatment of people with mental illness. Numerous examples of this are found throughout her *Memorial to the Legislature of Massachusetts, 1843*, which was reprinted in Rosen, Clark, and Kivitz (1976).

[5] During this period, humane treatment was often referred to as "moral treatment" (Whitaker, 2002).

[6] The importance of analyzing how the members of marginalized groups are depicted in popular culture is recognized by many national advocacy groups. GLAAD, for example, evaluates media portrayals of individuals who are gay, lesbian, transgender, or bisexual. The National Alliance on Mental Illness engages in the same type of analysis related to the framing of issues related to people with mental illness. There are many other examples of such initiatives.

[7] A good example of this is disability-related legislation. Those lawmakers who were primarily involved in ensuring passage of the Americans with Disabilities Act, for example, had almost to a person (Ted Kennedy, Bob Dole, Tom Harkin) experienced disability in their own family (O'Brien, 2004; Shapiro, 1993). This is also true of most important disability-related policies both before and since passage of the act.

several metaphors to describe when the time may be right for various policies to successfully navigate the political process. Alongside the metaphor of the policy window, which may open for only a brief time, he also used the wave metaphor, noting that advocates are like surfers who need to be prepared to get on the wave as soon as it arrives because it will not wait for them and will soon be gone (p. 165).

The presumption that legislators normally hold is that public funding should not be provided for social services, particularly during a period in which increasing taxes is anathema to the public as well as politicians. Political influence comes in two ways. The first and most important, at least in the current political climate, is through fund-raising and the provision of large sums of money to legislators to support their campaigns. Nonprofit agencies and social work professionals are themselves seldom in a position to make much of an impact through this route. The second way to influence the process, however, is through grassroots lobbying. This avenue is always available to social workers. It is unfortunately true that many of those who complain most vociferously that politicians only pay attention to large corporations and groups with massive sums of money have themselves not engaged in efforts to get to know their elected representatives and personally lobby for their cause. This must change if social workers are to become successful players in the policy arena. State-level legislators are in particular usually quite responsive to constituents. This is beneficial for social workers because over the past few decades, the states have become increasingly important in policy implementation and service provision.

IMPORTANCE OF METAPHORS IN SOCIAL POLICY

The ability of political stakeholders to control, manage, and wield words, images, and stories to present a desired means of framing a social problem or community subgroup is an important precursor to gaining or preserving power and control in relation to social policy issues. Because both linguistic and conceptual metaphors are frequently used to frame a social problem or group in a way that is desired by a specific constituency or important group or institution or to maintain the status quo, they have a great deal of influence in the policy arena. The significance of such perceptual frames can, for example, be easily gauged by perusing the *Congressional Record* when a controversial issue or proposed policy is discussed, especially when a degree of social control of a marginalized or stigmatized group is a potential policy solution. Such discussions are often laced with picturesque terminology and potent and often fear-inducing metaphors to further a desired perspective from which to view the problem (for examples, see Annas, 1995; Ellwood, 1995; Voss, Kennet, Wiley, & Schooler, 1992).

Selling Policy with Metaphors

Legislators and other political stakeholders have long known the importance of rhetoric and metaphors in selling various policy positions. George Lakoff (1996) has argued that a primary reason for the rising support of Republicans at the national level over the past few decades has been their use of language. Frank Luntz is certainly the most well-known rhetorical strategist among Republicans, and he helped fashion the Contract with America, which swept Republicans into office in the House in 1994. In his 2007 book *Words that Work,* Luntz describes his work in both the political and the commercial–industrial sectors. In fact, there is much carryover between the two, because selling policy positions is not that much different than selling products.[8] Luntz primarily used focus groups, in which he analyzed volunteers' response to a variety of terms and phrases related to political issues (Ball, 2014). Even subtle differences in terminology, he noted, can sway support for a position, and Luntz contended that "those who define the debate will determine the outcome" (p. 170). Many of the terms that Luntz created constitute the standard rhetoric of conservative politicians and lobbyists. Although the term "estate tax," for example, may bring to mind luxurious mansions and grounds and great wealth (which should be taxed), the term "death tax" (describing the same policy) fosters the perception that the government is getting people's money even after their lives have ended. Thus, the latter term is almost exclusively used by those who oppose the tax. Luntz's rhetorical recommendations (as well as those of others who have entered this rapidly growing and lucrative field) have been warmly embraced by politicians and other stakeholders over the past few decades.

---

[8] In fact, because much money is made from the political solutions that are signed into law, one can argue that policies can really be viewed as a type of product, and political stances can be perceived as a form of marketing.

It is interesting to note that not only do politicians generously pepper their speeches and writings with metaphors, but so too do other legislative and judicial bodies. As Cunningham-Parmeter (2011) described in great detail, even the Supreme Court, which one might think is the most objective and fair law-making body and thus not given to hyperbole or propagandist language, frequently supports its decisions using metaphors. As he noted, the court's recent decisions related to restrictive immigration laws include much of the same fear-based rhetoric that can be found in general discussions about the issue, in particular in relation to illegal immigrants. He contended that the

> metaphors floating in our minds determine our linguistic choices, which in turn affect social discourse and ultimately social action. Thus, how we *think* metaphorically affects how we *talk* about problems, and the *solutions* we formulate in response to those problems. (p. 1548)

As George Lakoff (1996) contended, those policymakers who are best able to use linguistic and conceptual metaphors in framing issues are those most apt to garner public support for their positions. For example, in her book *Grim Fairy Tales: The Rhetorical Construction of American Welfare Policy*, communications professor Lisa Gring-Pemble (2003) discussed at length how a pejorative framing of those in poverty paved the way for the development of a harsh welfare reform proposal in 1996's Temporary Assistance for Needy Families legislation. Particular images and "social constructions are manipulated and used by public officials, the media, and the groups themselves. New target groups are created, and images are developed for them; old groups are reconfigured or new images created" (Schneider & Ingram, 1993, p. 342; see also Landau, Keefer, & Rothschild, 2014).

Those individuals, groups, and institutions that foster specific negative stereotypical framings of marginalized groups and social issues do so in large part to advance their own ideological positions and political and economic standing. The metaphors discussed later in this book, therefore, often play a dual role: both supporting these existing negative stereotypes and at the same time buttressing the entrenched ideological positions of those who stand to profit, economically, politically, or otherwise, by publicly embracing such images.

One of the issues that people do not like to discuss in relation to oppression, discrimination, and social control measures is that there is often more than a little money to be made by entrenched interests in developing or maintaining such practices. When African Americans, for example, were relegated to very defined, highly congested areas of cities through restrictive covenant agreements, landlords were able to charge outrageous rents for apartments because potential residents were not allowed to move to other areas of the city (Comstock, 1912). This purposeful manipulation of supply and demand served the interests not only of white homeowners, but also of landlords, developers, and local businesses. Many similar examples of the close relationship between profit making and prejudice can be noted.

Risks of Oversimplification

A particular benefit of metaphor use in the policy arena, Schön (1979) added, is that metaphors may vastly simplify very "complex, uncertain, and indeterminate" situations (also see Semino, 2008). This is similar to what was noted previously in relation to metaphoric explanations to the lay public about technological or medical innovations. Much of what happens in the political arena is the result of an extraordinarily complicated series of interwoven events and personal, institutional, economic, resource, and international relationships. Operating in an era in which they are constantly besieged by stimuli related to a wide variety of social and political issues, however, the general public is not likely to devote much attention to the details. Metaphors and symbols are therefore used as shortcuts "to guide their political decisions" (Bougher, 2012; also see McBeth, Jones, & Shanahan, 2014). The decision to go to war in Iraq, for example, was symbolized for many by Colin Powell holding up a vial of yellowcake uranium in a speech to the United Nations. In addition to supplying presumably rational explanations for a decision to go to war, people will invoke a host of metaphors to vilify the enemy and present the battle as a necessary means of maintaining national pride and ensuring self-preservation (Keen, 1986).[9] As Lakoff (2014) noted in his book *Don't Think of an Elephant,* the George W. Bush administration had particular

---

[9] A somewhat similar example in which a staged image had much importance in relation to social policy was George H. W. Bush holding up a bag of crack cocaine in a televised speech. Bush said the drug was purchased by an undercover agent right outside the White House. Reinarman and Levine (1995) noted that the sale was set up by officials in an effort to support the contention that crack was available everywhere. These officials actually had some difficulty finding a seller who would agree to come to the area. It made for great television, however, and fostered public support of the War on Drugs.

political reasons for framing the post-9/11 fight against terrorism as a form of war rather than as a response to a criminal conspiracy.[10]

As noted earlier, the importance of linguistic and image-based metaphors in social policy can also be gauged by a cursory perusal of recent policy debates and the various rhetorical ways in which issues are differentially framed by those with opposing views of the issue. A seemingly simple difference such as that between illegal immigrants and undocumented immigrants can be a huge factor in how people feel about a policy (Chomsky, 2014). It is instructive, although in no way surprising, that those who favor policies such as border walls and deportation virtually always use the former descriptor (or "alien," or an equivalent derogatory term), and human rights advocates always use the latter.[11] More important, a contention that I return to repeatedly in this book is that the "distance between the linguistic dehumanization of a people and their actual suppression and extermination is not great; it is but a small step" (Bosmajian, 1983, p. 29).[12]

As noted in chapter 1, metaphors are an important component of the policy process not only because they can identify the way in which important stakeholders believe problems should be viewed, and thus the proper policy response, but also because they provide a potent means of evoking "strong emotional responses in listeners" (Ellwood, 1995). The denigration of various groups may relate to fears such as the loss of bodily integrity or possibility of physical invasion by contaminants; threats to personal safety or the safety of one's children; latent gender constructs; and, as noted previously, various manifestations of disgust or repugnance (Douglas, 1984; W. I. Miller, 1997). In the context of social policy, metaphors can certainly be viewed as a form of subconscious emotional manipulation (Charteris-Black, 2011, p. 44), and indeed this is among the more important reasons why social workers and other allies for social justice need to be able to understand their influence. As William I. Miller (1997) wrote, "Some emotions, among which disgust and its close cousin contempt are the most prominent, have intensely political significance" (p. 8).

---

[10] In fact, the administration used either war or criminal metaphors to fit the occasion. Incursion into other nations fit the latter framing, for example, whereas the continued detention of prisoners at Guantanamo Bay outside the confines of the Geneva Convention fit the former.

[11] To draw on another well-known contemporary example, many people who support the Patient Protection and Affordable Care Act (2010) do not like Obamacare, although they are one and the same.

[12] For an interesting contemporary example, also related to the immigration debate, see J. Lederer's (2013) article related to the use of the term "anchor babies."

METAPHORS AND THE SOCIAL CONSTRUCTION OF PROBLEMS

If, then, social policy substantively influences social work practice and indeed even the continued existence and organizational health of agencies within the community, and policy is in large part directed by metaphors, social workers who are unaware of how metaphors are used in the policy arena are devoid of an important instrument in their professional toolbox. Enhanced knowledge of metaphor use in policy, moreover, can benefit students' and employees' ability to assess and understand the metaphors that clients use in the treatment setting. The converse is also true. Awareness of how various terms, images, and phrases are used in one sphere informs the ability to analyze them elsewhere.

Problem Setting

In addition to the various rationales I have described for social workers to be engaged in deconstructing metaphors and policy rhetoric, it is crucial to note that the front end of this process dictates what follows in its wake. Although social workers are frequently focused on problem solving within the political arena, they need to understand the importance of problem setting, or the various ways in which problems are presented in the first place (Bougher, 2012, p. 147). Once a particular framing is widely embraced, the policy options that follow it seem to be simple common sense, because such images "impinge on all aspects of design, including selection of goals, targets, tools, and implementation strategies" (Schneider & Ingram, 1993, p. 345). Social workers who advocate within the policy process often waste a great deal of time and effort and become highly frustrated because they focus on policy change without paying enough attention to how the problem or group has been socially constructed in the first place or the preexisting presumptions legislators or other stakeholders have about the issue.

To reiterate an important point, people often make logical arguments when legislators have emotion- or value-based reasons for supporting or opposing various policies, and that is a recipe for failure. To quote Schneider and Ingram (1993), "Social construction of target populations is an important, often overlooked, political phenomenon that should take its place in the study of public policy by political scientists" (p. 334).

A correlation can be made between the front end of the policy process and the assessment and problem identification stages of social work treatment. If a social worker assesses a problem incorrectly in the first place, it is likely that she or he will design a poor treatment approach and waste a great deal of effort in working with the client. Just as social workers too often feel compelled to jump ahead and treat the individual or group before engaging in adequate assessment, so too it is with engagement in the policy arena. I would contend that the vast majority of energy and resources the social work community devotes to policy engagement needs to be directed to accurately understanding how the problem or group in question has been socially constructed, in part through metaphors and rhetoric, and understanding which particular stakeholders are apt to gain from that image and the policy approach with which it dovetails. Change is generally possible only when these dynamics are understood.

Typifications and Public Policy

Joel Best (1995) and Donileen Loseke (2003) have both discussed the importance of constructing social problems in particular ways to benefit certain stakeholders and guide policy formulation and funding down a specific pathway. Both of these authors discuss typifications, or constructions of problems that are designed to augment a certain image or picture of the problem in the minds of the public. These stereotyped images support a preferred view of the problem that lends itself to a specific policy response.

As noted in the Introduction, metaphor analysis relates to social constructionism. Loseke (2003) has written that social constructionist "perspectives encourage us to take words seriously because even the most simple words (*particularly* the most simple words) are categories for *entire systems of meaning*" (p. 16). At any given time, she noted, people can concern themselves with a multitude of different social problems, and so problem stakeholders (who often include social workers and agencies, of course) must compete with one another for public attention, and the typifications that are developed, and from which policy may be derived, are not necessarily an accurate depiction of the problem, but one that will draw attention when viewed within the constructs of the vast social problem marketplace.

Best (1995) described claims makers as those individuals who are invested in a particular social issue and its treatment and therefore attempt to put forth a compelling definition of the need for particular policies and resources. He noted that such people "inevitably characterize problems in particular ways: They emphasize some aspects and not others, they promote specific orientations, and they focus on particular causes and advocate particular solutions" (p. 9). Claims makers must often reframe or repackage a problem to draw attention to it, and "claims that succeed reflect a particular construction of the problem, which comes to be seen as authoritative, and those claimsmakers achieve 'ownership' of the problem" (Lowney & Best, 1995, p. 34).

Similar to these authors, Nancy Fraser (1989) discussed the competition that takes place over the identification of needs. In her book *Unruly Practices,* she considered need identification from a feminist perspective and assessed how various group needs are framed. Because people's perception of need, especially in relation to other alternative needs, is driven largely by problem or group framing and considerations of deservedness and power relationships, she viewed need interpretation as being largely a political matter that is influenced by various constructionist perspectives.

This does give rise to an intriguing ethical issue that social workers and other policy stakeholders may face. On the one hand, they are compelled to engage in a degree of propagandizing of the social problems they deal with to justify their services. Horror stories related to child abuse, domestic violence, drug addiction, and so forth are an integral part of social work because social workers need to demonstrate, as clearly as possible, the damage that such problems can cause. It could be argued, however, that social workers are exploiting these examples and unfairly using the worst scenarios as typical. This could further lead to an awfulization of the problem and enhance the stigma related to it. There really seems to be no good answer to this inherent double bind, although it is obviously important that social workers be cautious about how they use client experiences, even if informed consent is obtained and privacy is maintained.

In chapters 4 and 5, I further delineate some of these typifications, or stereotyped images, in particular those that directly relate to vulnerable populations and the social policy initiatives that are designed to restrict the rights or otherwise impinge on the opportunities afforded to such people. A cottage industry of claims makers and corporate or media stakeholders will often develop to institutionalize a particular mode of responding to the problem based on the prevailing metaphor or metaphors. As alluded to earlier, there is much cross-fertilization in how such images are designed and implemented at different times and in relation to different target groups, as well as the various corporate and other groups that profit from the creation and dissemination of denigrating images.

4
Metaphors That Dehumanize and Objectify

*What we forget is that the [feebleminded] woman is not responsible.
She can no more live in accordance with the conventions of society
than the cats and dogs in the street.*
—Goddard (1912, p. 1853)

*It is a no more difficult task to detect poorly built, defective
or broken down human beings than to recognize a cheap
or defective automobile.*
—Ellis Island physician (as cited in Kraut, 1994, p. 63)

Treating others in an animalistic fashion or referring to them as animal-like or as a lower form of humanity is among the most frequent modes of denigrating minority groups.[1] Objectification constitutes a similar form of degradation. Both themes hold the other out as a lesser person (or entity); therefore, those who invoke the metaphor place themselves in a higher relative position (Haslam, 2006). If one thinks back to the quotation from chapter 2 that depicted social workers as romping in sandboxes (Bethell, 1993), in addition to linguistic metaphors designed to infantilize and animalize social workers (as children or cats), there is a clear cognitive metaphor at play that relates to the relative valuation of various people. The implication is that the writer, and by association those who are similar to the writer, is of higher value than social workers. As a more advanced entity, the writer, like a parent or other authority figure, presumes the right to judge, identify, castigate, and demean those he or she considers lesser.

---

[1]Some portions of this chapter were previously published in O'Brien (2009).

Both objectification and animalization imply that the targets of the metaphor can be controlled, either because they, like animals, have less intellectual capacity and diminished ability, and thus tend to make poor decisions, or because, like objects or domesticated animals, they can be used for the good of those who might benefit from controlling them. As one might presume, this latter rationale is couched as what is good for society at large rather than good for the controlling class. As I introduced in chapter 2, and revisit later in this chapter's discussion of altruistic rationales, oppressors may even contend that they are engaging in self-sacrifice through an oppressive interpersonal relationship (for example, the white man's burden).

I should note at the outset that some animal or object metaphors may have a neutral or even a positive connotation (Haslam, Loughnan, & Sun, 2011). In the United States, for example, the eagle is seldom used to foster a negative image. As a national symbol, it is proud, strong, vigilant, and beautiful. A nation at war with the United States, however, would be expected to depict the negative attributes of the symbol, with the eagle presented as a ravenous and heartless predator intent on swooping down and destroying weaker, innocent animals.

Another example of a positive animal metaphor is the wolf or lion in Nazi Germany. As Sax (2000) noted, the wolf was presented by the Nazis as a fierce predator that had not been weakened through domestication. Hitler so admired the animal that his own nickname was the Wolf, which was particularly apropos because the Jews had long been symbolized by National Socialists as sheep. The Nazis also used the lion metaphor to characterize their soldiers (Keen, 1986). Fierce, proud, and dominating, this image contrasted dramatically with the rat metaphor that they frequently used to denigrate Jews; lowly, associated with waste, filth, disease, and contagion, the rat hides in the shadows and only strikes when its target lets down its guard.[2]

To properly deconstruct the meaning behind the metaphor, then, one may need to understand the cultural context in which it is used, including the social, economic, or political goals of the speaker or writer. For example, an employer who refers to an employee as working like a machine (an object metaphor) can mean this in a positive way (an efficient,

---

[2]Of course the lion also often sneaks up on its prey. That characteristic, however, does not fit well with the other metaphoric attributes of the lion, especially as the Nazis wanted to portray the animal, so it was easily discarded.

Metaphors That Dehumanize and Objectify 57

hard worker who requires few breaks) or a negative way (mechanistic, easily exploited, and uncreative). Consider also the anchor metaphor. An anchor can be a stabilizing force that keeps a person from drifting, or it can be an object that limits that person's ability to progress or move forward (O'Brien, 2011a). In most cases, however—especially in the political arena—it does not take a great deal of contextualization to understand the meaning behind a particular metaphor. Indeed, one of the benefits of metaphors, and one of the reasons they are so frequently used, is that they generally require little consideration to understand their meaning and, again, may even be designed to work in a largely subconscious fashion. One does not have to contemplate too long to understand that the term "anchor baby" has a decidedly negative connotation (J. Lederer, 2013), especially when it is used by those opposing undocumented immigrants.[3]

Although culturally specific elements may play into how various metaphors are interpreted, in many cases object, animal, and other pejorative metaphors are perceived in a similar way across differing cultures (Talibinejad & Dastjerdi, 2005). Rats and low animals such as roaches, bugs, and vermin are almost always perceived negatively, and thus connections are often made between them and target group members (Berke, 2000; Metrick-Chen, 2012). As Daniel Goldhagen (2009) noted in *Worse than War,* his book on genocides and the shared factors that connect various genocidal programs, similar pejorative images were an instrumental part of genocidal programs in very divergent cultures during different time periods. D. L. Smith (2011) said that "although the details vary from culture to culture and epoch to epoch, the dehumanizing imagination consistently produces astonishingly similar results" (p. 156).

Rather than simply providing an expansive laundry list of oppressive periods and how animal metaphors or similar forms of dehumanization or objectification have been used, in this chapter I look at important thematic elements contained within these metaphors, or major modes of denigration, that cut across various alarm periods. I especially focus on themes that have continued importance for social justice and the social work profession. An encyclopedic account of animal and object metaphors, as well as those discussed in the following chapter, would be well beyond the scope of this work. Several authors have provided

---

[3]Similarly, a metaphor of more recent vintage used against immigrants is chain migration. Chains have an obvious negative connotation, as used in prisons, in relation to slavery, forms of torture, and so forth.

extensive examples of the various ways in which these themes have appeared, as well as their relationship to particular measures of social control (for example, see Brennan, 1995; Ewen & Ewen, 2006; Keen, 1986; Noël, 1994; D. L. Smith, 2011).

ANIMAL METAPHORS AND DEGREES OF HUMANNESS

Animalistic terminology, descriptions, or conceptual images are frequently used to highlight negative stereotyped characteristics of target group members (Haslam, 2006). As Henri Zuckier (1996) noted, in extreme cases propagandists may even question where the boundary line that demarcates humans from nonhuman animals is located and whether target groups fall inside or outside this line (also see Ritvo, 1995). Indeed, the term "marginalized" itself relates to this perception that group members might not be considered to be full-fledged members of the human community but rather exist on the margins or outlying boundaries of the community, nation, race, or even species. This obviously makes such people vulnerable, because the closer they lie to a boundary line, the easier it is to move them over it. If such groups can be accorded nonhuman or quasi-human status, they can be treated with less than the full complement of human rights or given less than the full degree of consideration. Because social workers and other allies for social justice often work with people who exist on the margins of society, this issue is particularly apropos to their work.

Those considered to be on the margins of society are also frequently targets of suspicion. Their true loyalty may be questioned. They may attempt to furtively cross societal borders (African Americans attempting to pass as white Americans, Jews changing their names so as to not have their businesses boycotted by anti-Semites, people with disabilities hiding their condition because of fears of discrimination, Japanese immigrants owning land under American names, and so forth), or they may try to metaphorically contaminate the normal members of society through such means as miscegenation or sexual assault. In cases such as the spread of HIV or other sexually transmitted diseases, actual physical contamination of the community may also be feared in addition to metaphoric contamination. As introduced earlier and further discussed in the next chapter in relation to psychological contagion and courtesy stigma, working with people on the margins of society may indeed serve to conceptually place social workers themselves somewhat closer to the outer boundaries of the community.

Scale of Humanity, the Missing Link, and the Beast

Social movements often implicitly include elements of a scale of humanity on which various gradations of humans can be gauged on the basis of racial, personal, behavioral, or other traits or statuses, such as economic standing. Thus, even if all members of the species are accepted as actual human beings, some may be denied certain rights or opportunities on the basis of their placement on such a scale (Ritvo, 1995). This graded view of the species explains in part why it is frequently the ape or monkey that is used as a metaphor for the devalued target group (Ewen & Ewen, 2006; Noël, 1994).

Numerous writings that supported race-based segregation during the early part of the 20th century (as well as slavery before this) drew on racial anthropological thinking that placed African Americans as a missing link between normal humans and simians, or simply as a beast (Gould, 1981). One astonishing example of this is a book published in 1900 by Charles Carroll titled *The Negro a Beast*. Over the course of its 350-plus pages, Carroll laid out an argument, based on the Christian Bible, physiological comparisons, and various forms of pseudoscience, that African Americans were much closer to the great apes than they were to white Americans. Lott (1999) wrote that many of the minstrel shows of the 1800s featured "ape images to represent black people" (p. 12; also see Strausbaugh, 2006).

Another example of the missing link theme centered on people who were assumed to have intellectual or other types of disabilities, with many freak shows from the late 19th and early 20th centuries depicting such individuals as being representative of lost tribes, whose members combined human and apelike qualities. Some of these freak shows juxtaposed racial and disability-related antipathy because they displayed people with microcephaly or other forms of disability as missing links who were found in exotic, more primitive locales (Bogdan, 1988; Fiedler, 1978).[4]

---

[4]Perhaps the most infamous description of the use of people with disabilities in sideshows was the movie *Freaks*, which was made in 1932 (Browning, 1932). For an interesting overview of the movie, see chapter 2 of A. M. Smith's (2012) *Hideous Progeny*.

Similarly, Trent (1998) noted that the 1904 St. Louis World's Fair set up a number of anthropological displays in which visitors could observe primitive peoples in their natural environments, not at all unlike a human zoo. The term "Mongoloid," an early descriptor for people with Down syndrome, arose out of the belief that various intellectual disabilities were the result of atavism, or the ability of people who were lower on the racial–species hierarchy to have children who were indicative of an earlier phase of human evolution (Gould, 1980; Wright, 2004).[5]

Cesare Lombroso, an early Italian criminologist, wrote toward the end of the 1900s that criminals constituted an atavistic throwback to an earlier, more primitive stage of human evolution. Such atavism, he argued, "may go back far beyond the savage, even to the brutes themselves" (Lombroso, 1911/1968, p. 367). To Lombroso, hereditary or born criminals resembled "lemurs and rodents" in some respects. Epileptics, too, he noted, many of whom he classified as criminalistic, also possessed many of the characteristics of "instinctive animalism."

During the early decades of the 20th century, Lombroso's (1911/1968) concepts were embraced by many American criminologists and eugenicists. Certainly there remains an undercurrent of primitivism or animalism that continues to define criminals in popular culture. Often the initial response one has to a particularly horrid crime is that the perpetrator is an animal or a beast.[6] In a sense, though, this is highly pejorative toward animals, because humans (at least some) have shown themselves to be capable of crimes that are much more horrendous and cruel than any animal would perpetrate. Social workers and others who work in criminal justice settings need to maintain awareness of the degree to which they (or the settings in which they work) embrace the bestial image of criminals and the impact this may have on treatment and rehabilitation efforts.

---

[5]Because many of those who believed in this concept during the 19th century assumed that these evolutionary stages could be gauged through the relative primitivism of the race that was most similar to the deformed child, Mongoloids, for example, who now are classified as children with Down syndrome, were taken as falling between the higher white and lower African types (see chapter 15 of Gould's 1980 *The Panda's Thumb*). For early race classification schemes, see Gould's (1981) *Mismeasure of Man* or J. S. Haller Jr.'s (1971) *Outcasts from Evolution: Scientific Attitudes of Racial Inferiority, 1859–1900*.

[6]To revisit a point made in chapter 2, Thibodeau and Boroditsky (2011), in their study of the relationship between metaphors and decision making, found that the specific policy recommendations favored by subjects depended in part on how the problem was framed through metaphor priming. Those subjects who viewed crime as a beast (and thus perceived criminals as bestial) were more apt to support harsher control measures.

Animalization and Social Control

Much has been written about the various ways in which animalization of marginalized racial groups was used to support not only slavery but additional measures of social control, both in the United States and elsewhere. For example, the belief that African Americans were only happy when they were domesticated and controlled by a kindly, more intelligent master would live on well past the Emancipation Proclamation. Manifest Destiny, colonialism, imperialism, and the white man's burden were supported through the notion that less evolved cultures could not properly use their resources or govern their people (Horsman, 1981). Numerous additional examples exist of the rights of vulnerable groups being abrogated because of their status as less developed or endowed beings. For not only African Americans, but also women, voting was not allowed for much of the nation's history, in part because of the assumption that a certain level of intelligence was required of electors, and they fell short on this count. People with feeblemindedness or mental retardation were forcibly sterilized or institutionalized because it was believed that they could not control their animal passions or instincts (O'Brien, 2003b); Chinese Americans were barred from the country or forced out of various cities on the West Coast because they were thought to live such a basic, primitivistic existence that American workers could not compete with them in the labor force; and so forth (Perkins, 1906).

It is important to note that in many of these examples, as well as others one might think of, what might otherwise be interpreted as a positive quality is turned on its head to fit the oppressive narrative. Considering the final example of Chinese Americans, for example, American workers' inability to compete with them was a constant refrain, and it was also used later against both Japanese Americans on the West Coast and Jews and other new (Eastern and Southern European) immigrants on the East Coast. These groups supposedly lived such frugal lives in primitive hovels that they lowered the standard of living for Americans, such that the latter could not effectively compete with them (Ellis, 1923; Frazier, 1923). This was an ironic criticism coming from a nation of people who expressed great pride that their own ancestors started from the bottom and went through constant hardships to give their children a better life. This theme has carried forward to the current day, when undocumented immigrants are often criticized for taking American jobs, lowering both the overall pay scale and living standards (Chomsky, 2014).

Hierarchies of Humanity and Worthiness

The Great Chain of Being, a philosophical construct for centuries, has been an important mode of classifying and evaluating different castes of humans. Beginning with the simplest single-cell organisms, each species was thought to constitute a link that was connected to another in a massive chain that eventually ended in the highest possible entity, God. The Chain of Being held that the lowest members of the human species connected with the most evolved nonhuman animals, and in particular the great apes, and that the highest members of the species connected with spiritual entities. As one might guess, physicality and emotionality were perceived as largely reserved for those entities on the bottom of the human scale (African Americans, Native Americans, women, people with intellectual disabilities or mental illness), whereas reason[7] was the central characteristic of the highest group (Gelb, 1995; Lovejoy, 1966; O'Brien, 2003b, 2011b). From the hysterical female of the 1910s to the current depiction of the gay drama queen, people still tend to perceive highly emotional groups to be not only less in control of themselves, but also less capable of higher level reasoning and self-governance (Rodríguez, 2009). A central tenet of scales or hierarchies such as the Great Chain of Being is that the values that serve to differentiate groups are those values that the group in power hold to be most important or believe that they and those like them hold in abundance.

For many scholars, it has been the intellect that places humans above other animals, so the taxonomic placement of people with mental retardation and mental illness has frequently been a source of contention by philosophers and other scholars. Martha Nussbaum (2006) wrote that

> Kant's conception of the person lies in a long tradition that goes straight back to the Greek and Roman Stoics, in which personhood is identified with reason . . . and in which reason, so construed, is taken to be a feature of human beings that sets them sharply apart from nonhuman animals and from their own animality. (p. 130)

---

[7]Although reason is generally an indicator of higher status and a platform for judgmental attitudes in relation to lower beings, it is certainly true that reason is not necessarily defined as being intellectual or highly educated. Nazi Germany included intellectuals in the umbrella of undesirables, and the form of reason that was embraced was common sense. Those who agreed with the goals and methods of Hitlerism, moreover, displayed such common sense. One certainly does not need to search too long in current political discussions in the United States to find politicians who derogate intellectualism as the refuge of egghead professors who live far outside the boundaries of the real America and lack true common sense.

Even some animal rights literature currently seems to diminish the status of people with cognitive disabilities (whether or not this is its intent) by comparing their intellectual capacity with that of nonhumans. The well-known Princeton philosopher Peter Singer, for example, contended that chimpanzees should not be used in medical experiments if humans with similar reasoning capacity (people with severe intellectual disabilities) are not similarly used. To use the former but not the latter, he contended, is speciesism, or discrimination based simply on species membership (Cavalieri & Singer, 1993; O'Brien, 2003b; Ryan, 2014; Singer, 1975).

Although most people might contend that these human–animal juxtapositions are the stuff of ancient history and have little impact today, a fascinating 2008 study by Phillip Goff, Eberhardt, Williams, and Jackson shed light on the fact that such myths continue to live on, at least in the recesses of people's subconscious. In a series of experiments, these authors demonstrated that ape images that were displayed on a screen with pixilation gradually enhanced were more likely to be recognized as apes at an earlier stage of projection if subjects had been primed with images of African American faces before they had to decide what the projected images were. Priming with images of white faces did not have the same impact. These authors are correct in noting that most people pick up this connection in very subtle ways throughout their lives, and they contended that an inherent view of African Americans as subhuman partially accounts for their differential treatment in criminal justice and other settings (Goff et al., 2008; also see Lott, 1999; Maass et al., 2014). Drawing attention to the largely subconscious nature of such reactions, in 2006 Harris and Fiske conducted brain scans of subjects while stereotypical images were presented to them. According to these authors, people who were viewed as both hostile and incompetent, such as homeless people and drug addicts, registered a response in the area of the brain that coincides with disgust reactions.

It is important for helping professionals to be aware of the role of cognitive capacity (or presumptions thereof) in how they perceive and interact with people who may have a diagnosis of mental illness, developmental disability, or age-related cognitive impairments. As further discussed in the "Infantilization" section, people frequently respond to such people as, if not subhuman, at least as individuals who cannot make good decisions and need paternalistic direction. Moreover, the issue of disability spread comes into play, in which one may assume that individuals with certain physical disabilities, such as cerebral palsy, also have cognitive or intellectual deficits and as a result of this misperception treat them in a demeaning, childlike manner (Livneh, 1991).

OTHER FORMS OF ANIMALIZATION

Those animals that are chosen to represent target groups are frequently either harmful (snakes, wolves, octopi), insignificant (ants, roaches), or both (parasites, rats, and termites). Often the stereotyped characteristic of the group that is the basis for their identification or control portends the use of a specific animal (Silaški, 2013). During the immigration restriction movement (1900–1925), the public was repeatedly warned that illegal immigrants, breeding like rabbits, threatened to take over the nation if their numbers were not controlled (O'Brien, 2003a).[8] Among a host of pejorative metaphors, Nazi thinking portrayed Jews as infectious rats or poisonous snakes that cowardly hid in the dark and threatened to spread disease and death among the population (Keen, 1986). According to Ruth Sidel (2000), during the debate over welfare reform a Florida legislator compared welfare recipients to domesticated animals who had become dependent on the aid of people and could no longer fend for themselves. In conservative literature, the welfare mother has frequently been compared to a particularly disgusting, lazy, greedy animal: the brood sow (Placek & Hendershot, 1974).

Small animals may especially be used to provide an image that is analogous to the marginalized group because such animals are themselves viewed in an objectivist light. In other words, many of those who oppose animal testing on dogs or monkeys might be more apt to allow it on mice because the former are not only more insignificant with respect to size but are also considered to be less individualistic or, to reiterate a point made earlier, seem to function on a lower intellectual plane and thus are less endowed with a spiritual nature.

Emotional and aesthetic attributes (for example, perceived empathy for other members of the species, attention to one's young, curiosity, cuteness, sliminess, cleanliness, cruel nature) may also be imposed on particular animals, making them more or less apt to be used as a point of

---

[8] The prodigious procreator image not only puts forth the view that the target group is threatening to take over the nation through expansive numbers, but also serves to dehumanize women by objectifying them as immoral, instinctual, and highly sexualized.

comparison in specific situations (Blatt, 1970).[9] Haslam et al. (2011) studied subjects' response to many different animal metaphors and found that the degree of offensiveness pertained largely to whether specific animals were disliked and whether they "were seen as dehumanizing the target" group (p. 318) to which they had been compared.

INTERSECTION WITH OTHER METAPHOR THEMES

Animalization metaphors at times overlap with both war and organism metaphors, which are described in the next chapter. The enemy in war is frequently presented as a particularly rapacious, sneaky, or cruel animal, as Keen (1986) pointed out in *Faces of the Enemy*. As discussed earlier, animalistic metaphors that relate to contagion (rats, lice, vermin, and so forth) connect disgusting animal images to people's fear of contagion and potential threats to their bodily integrity. In fact, the three metaphors are often interconnected with one another, because people engage in public health battles against either contagious disease or the animals that spread contagion.

Thus, as I pick up on in the next chapter's discussion of the organism metaphor, the denigration of devalued or threatening groups is often framed as a comparison with pests or parasites (Inda, 2000; Musolff, 2010). Edmund Russell (1996) discussed not only the rhetorical connections among lice, rodents, or pests and enemy combatants in World War II, but also the fact that the science "of pest control sometimes became the science ... of war" (p. 1508), as chemical weapon development was carried over from exterminating bugs to killing humans. The pesticide Zyklon B, used for mass killing in the Holocaust, was originally developed, in weaker strength, to kill vermin and later to fumigate immigrants who entered the United States from Mexico (Romo, 2005). Shinozuka (2013) added that Japanese immigrants in California during the 1910s and 1920s were compared to Japanese beetles. Both were "toxic trespasser[s]" who sought to take over and exhaust American farmland. Immigrants

---

[9]There is a form of circular reasoning at play here. First, people anthropomorphize animals by imposing human attributes or motives on them (for example, pigs as lazy, slovenly, and self-centered), and then they impose the metaphoric animal identity onto specific people as a way of denigrating them ("she's just a pig") (Silaški, 2013). Kövecses (2010) wrote, "The only way these [animalistic] meanings can have emerged is that humans attributed human characteristics to animals and then reapplied these characteristics to humans" (p. 125).

especially are often derogated in this way, even in recent years. Bridget Anderson (2017) wrote that "one metaphoric trope that has emerged as particularly powerful in the coverage of the 2015 events [Syrian refugee crisis] is the migrant as invasive insect" (p. 8).

An interesting and creative example of the use of the parasite metaphor to dehumanize a target group was the use of the Succulina in the description of the Ishmaels, one of the more well-known of the eugenic family studies. This parasite lives off the crab, and Oscar McCulloch, the author of the family study, believed that it was an apt analogy to describe the degenerate Indiana family he was studying. Deutsch (2009) wrote that "the parable of the parasitic crustaceans would be almost comical if its social implications were not so disturbing. McCulloch firmly believed that he had discovered a 'history of similar degradation' in the Tribe of Ishmael" (p. 51). This family study is instructive in that it brought together a confluence of many derogatory tropes (filth, immorality, foreign origin, Islam and Native American influence), each of which furthered the dehumanization of the large extended family (also see Rafter, 1988).

One of the more interesting examples of the juxtaposition of pest and people for the purpose of denigrating the latter was the connection of African Americans in the American South with the boll weevil. Entering the country from Mexico, like other uninvited and unwanted guests, the boll weevil took over cotton land in the South in the first decade of the 20th century and therefore had a major impact on the Great Migration of African Americans to northern urban centers. Many writers of the time compared African Americans in the South to boll weevils, because both were said to be reliant on cotton crops,[10] reproduced exponentially, and threatened southern communities (Giesen, 2011; Shaffer, 1922). Eventually, some southern communities came to see the boll weevil as a godsend because it forced them to diversify crop production while at the same time diminishing their reliance on African American farm laborers, many of whom were forced to move northward (Giesen, 2011).

---

[10] As Giesen (2011) noted, one of the reasons why African Americans were more reliant on cotton crops than white farmers is that the former were not able to own their own land and thus worked as tenant farmers. They also could not procure the loans needed to begin producing other crops, such as peanuts.

Altruistic Metaphors

In many cases, control of an out-group by those in power, or a limitation of the rights provided to the former, may be rationalized through altruistic metaphors, which are primarily characterized by paternalistic rhetoric and the contention that those who support oppressive policies are acting on behalf of the target group. The controlling group or agent frames itself as a loving but firm parent, and those who are controlled are demeaned as children who require guidance and supervision. As noted previously, this metaphor was certainly very clear historically in rationalizing imperialism, control of Native American tribes, and other such actions, in which the residents of nondeveloped nations were presented as primitivistic groups that were unable to either access or wisely use the resources in their territories. They presumably did not have the capacity for self-governance, were unable to plan for the future, and had the intellectual capacity of children, at least as compared with more evolved Western standards. In another example, in 1904 one writer said of African Americans that they were "a mass of grown-up children from whom all the wholesome restraint found in slavery had been removed and nothing substituted. . . . They possessed grown-up desires and passions but only the judgment and will-power of children" (C. C. Smith, 1904, p. 728).

A central component of the paternalistic metaphor is the contention that those who oppress are acting in the best interests of their victims but that the latter are either too unintelligent, shortsighted, or self-absorbed to understand this. Subjugation, Lise Noël (1994) wrote, is viewed from this perspective as a means of protection:

> Far from finding satisfaction in the power he holds over the oppressed, the dominator feels it to be a burden, an additional responsibility weighing on his shoulders. He therefore sees the control he exercises as a duty more than a privilege. (p. 125)

Many examples can be found of altruistic arguments being invoked for the purpose of demeaning or disempowering vulnerable groups. Many of those who supported slavery argued that this was the natural role of blacks and that they would not be able to support themselves, or potentially even survive, if freed. It has also been contended that women's engaging in their natural roles as wife and mother was best for their mental health and that too much stimulation (for example, decision making, out-of-home work) would pose a grave risk to their sensitive natures. Japanese Americans needed to be interned to protect them from retribution from angry white Americans as a result of Pearl Harbor, and people with mental retardation who were forcibly sterilized were said to benefit from the procedure.

Regarding this last example, two of the leaders of the California eugenics program noted that the vast majority of women who were involuntarily sterilized in the course of this program were "pathetic in their expression of gratitude" (Gosney & Popenoe, 1929) for the procedure. Altruism in this case was said to be doubly beneficial because it was best for both the potential mothers and their never-born children. Given the importance of heredity to eugenicists, it was believed that such children would likely be feebleminded themselves and live a life of diminished value to both themselves and society.

In their most extreme application, altruistic metaphors may even be invoked to support the killing of vulnerable populations. Over the course of time, for example, many have supported the infanticide or mercy killing of people with severe disabilities under the guise of paternalism. In many cases, however, what constitutes a severe disability is in the eye of the beholder. It has often been argued, for example, that it would be horrible to live with such a condition and that people would welcome such actions if they were in such a situation. Consider, for example, the following quote in support of eugenically based euthanasia provided by an American eugenicist:

> The surest, the simplest, the kindest and most humane means for preventing reproduction among those whom we deem unworthy of this high privilege, is a *gentle, painless death;* and this should be administered not as a punishment, but as an expression of enlightened pity for the victims—too defective by nature to find true happiness in life—and as a duty toward the community and toward our own offspring.[11] (McKim, 1901, p. 188)

It is interesting that Helen Keller (1915) came out in support of euthanasia for newborns with intellectual disabilities. She wrote a letter to the editor

---

[11] As one might assume, it was the Nazis who engaged in the most extensive effort to sanitize murder (the word "sanitize" itself is a descriptive metaphor for a form of ethnic or racial cleansing) by presenting it as an honorable action. For example, they developed a series of motion pictures that were designed to depict the horrors of living with a severe disability. Humans were, they contended, more respectful of animals than of humans because humans had the decency to put animals out of their misery when the time came.

of the *New Republic* supporting a controversial Chicago physician who allowed such an infant to die rather than perform life-saving surgery (also see Pernick, 1996). In a 1938 article, American eugenicist William Lennox wrote of his support for euthanasia for "congenital idiots or monsters" who had "human form but [were] without human mind" (p. 457). He also supported research on new birth control procedures, noting that "Germany in time might have solved her Jewish problems in this way" (p. 461). Very shortly after this, euthanasia was presented to the public in Nazi Germany as a good death that saved its victims from a life of struggle and pain (Burleigh, 1994; Weindling, 2000).

Altruism and Religious Metaphors

The religious metaphor infuses religious rhetoric or symbolism into arguments for social control. Here the group in question is portrayed as evil, immoral, or detrimental to the spiritual foundations of the community. Those supporting the movement against the target group will often take pains to demonstrate that its goals or methods are in keeping with mainstream religious or moral precepts, and they may even attempt to exploit religious symbols or practices to support the movement or use existing religious networks to disseminate propaganda (O'Brien & Molinari, 2011; Wiggam, 1922). Charles Carroll (1900), for example, was not by any means the only segregationist writer to use the Bible to provide evidence that African Americans should be classified as subhuman entities.

In those societies in which freedom of religion is included in the spectrum of individual rights, overt discrimination against those belonging to minority religions is generally deemed to be inappropriate. Even in nations that laud religious freedom, however, persecution of those who are framed as operating outside normative religious boundaries may be acceptable and, in some cases, even presented as a duty. This is especially likely if those belonging to a minority religion, or who profess to be atheist or agnostic, can be perceived as challenging the precepts of the majority religion, especially if, as was the case with the various anti-Communist movements in the United States, they can be presented as engaging in a purposeful conspiracy to damage or destroy it (Hogan, 2009).

Even if target group members are not denigrated on overtly religious grounds, such as belonging to a minority religion, religious elements such as immorality or sinfulness often provide a foundation for their depreciation. Groups may be stereotyped as being intemperate, sexually promiscuous, unfettered by the moral code of the community, or, as is the case with an important current framing of Muslims, suspect because of their supposed alliances.

Social work itself obviously has a religious foundation of which social workers are justifiably proud; the profession developed in large part from religious-based service organizations, and such agencies remain an important component of the nation's social service delivery system. However, when it comes to providing services to others in need, there has always been a fine line between engaging in such activities out of empathy and a recognition of people's shared humanity and providing such services with patronizing or condescending motives. Even among social workers, certain religious or moral precepts have been used over the course of time to justify the depreciation or control of specific vulnerable populations. Religious artifacts or language may also be used as a way of describing devalued populations, social problems, or proposed solutions. Religion and morality are frequently used as vehicles to depreciate or patronize vulnerable populations. Gring-Pemble (2003), for example, discusses this in an analysis of the legislative discussions on Temporary Assistance for Needy Families:

> By invoking scripture and religious imagery, legislators could argue that their political preferences and policies were part of a higher, perhaps divine, plan. In this frame, legislators were above partisan politics and were acting morally and ethically. The religious imagery also cast doubt on the morality of welfare recipients. (p. 122)

Infantilization

Infantilization is a form of dehumanization frequently seen in social work practice that is similar to animalization. Here, adults are treated in a more childlike manner than is appropriate, based in part on assumptions that they are somewhat childlike or are associated with a group that carries this stereotype. Obviously, elderly people, and especially those with particular physical or cognitive impairments, are apt to be victims of infantilizing treatment, as are people with various types of disabilities, particularly intellectual or cognitive disabilities. When working with any of these groups, age-appropriate activities, material, and forms of engagement are important features of treatment.[12]

Marson and Powell (2014) discussed the infantilization of elderly people and drew on Erving Goffman's (1959, 1961, 1963) writings as a meaningful way to analyze geriatric treatment, particularly of those in nursing homes and other congregate care settings.[13] The roles or framings that people take on in differing circumstances or in response to different people (termed "impression management" by Goffman, 1959) are similar to metaphors, in that they tell a particular story about different people and who they are attempting to present themselves as, as well as how they are trying to negotiate their surroundings. As Marson and Powell noted, clients will often play whatever role they feel they must take on to derive the greatest benefit from their interaction with workers and to make their lives as stress free as possible while in the setting. People in nursing homes or other congregate care or geriatric facilities, for example, may not respond negatively to demeaning, childish treatment from workers because they are dependent on these same workers (perhaps for a long period of time) for all manner of necessities, conveniences, and privileges.

OBJECT METAPHOR

In the context of the object metaphor, impersonal items are used to highlight the presumed (usually negative) characteristics of the target group. The value of group members is not a given but may be based on their ability to perform a specific role, such as breeder, worker, or soldier. They may be viewed as interchangeable objects with little individual personality, and the target classification—disabled person, Communist sympathizer, Japanese, Jew—may be presented by those in power as their

---

[12] Even when the activities in which a client can engage are well below what would be expected for their age level, age-appropriate versions of those activities are available, especially through Internet sites that cater to such populations.

[13] I introduced Goffman in chapter 2, and his work is particularly important for the analysis of metaphor, especially in social work. His 1961 book on asylums compares total institutions, such as detention facilities or institutions, with a performance stage on which the various actors (professionals, clients, support staff) take on, even subconsciously, the accoutrements of the assumed role to which they are assigned. Much can be said about Goffman's analysis and the interaction between workers and clients, not only in total institutions but elsewhere. One key issue, though, is that for clients, social workers are viewed in a way that is circumscribed by the client's previous history with social service professionals and other authorities. One might even say that social workers themselves are viewed in a metaphoric way on the basis of this selective personal history.

master status, or principal identifying role. The earlier discussion of Goffman's writings provides a good segue into this metaphor theme because it supports the perception that people are often objectified by who they are (profession) or their role relationship to others (parent, spouse, child, and so forth).

The primary identifiers through which people are described, moreover, are often said to be largely unalterable, either through environmental factors or through their own efforts to change. During congressional hearings on Japanese internment, for example, one legislator supported interning not only recent Japanese immigrants, but all Japanese who were living on the West Coast, regardless of their length of residency in the country (which would be the eventual policy). He contended that "we cannot trust them. . . . Once a Jap always a Jap. You cannot change him. You cannot make a silk purse out of a sow's ear" ("Statement of Congressman Rankin," 1942, p. 1682).

As one might assume, because such people were not just foreign but indeed were taken to be incapable of ever being truly assimilated into the nation, they were particularly undesirable immigrants. In addition, because they (and their descendants) would always have a foreign essence, it was contended, one could never be sure where their true loyalties would lie.[14] Jewish Americans were perceived in much the same way during the first decades of the 20th century; many questioned whether their primary loyalty was toward their adopted homeland or to the cause of Zionism (*The International Jew*, 1920). Certainly the same can be said for the current perception many in this country have of Muslims, regardless of their immigration or naturalization status or even the length of time they have been in the United States.

Devaluation of Others

People want to believe that devalued people are fundamentally flawed for several reasons. First, their status is thus their own fault, rather than that of the culture or society; second, time or energy does not need to be put into rehabilitation efforts; and finally, failed efforts at rehabilitation can

---

[14] Although questions about the loyalty of Japanese Americans were especially raised after the Pearl Harbor bombing, this had been an ongoing concern of those on the West Coast who opposed Japanese migration for decades before World War II. A 1925 article that appeared in the *Literary Digest* magazine, for example, noted the following: "In the event of war between the United States and Japan, the Japanese element here [Hawaii] would side with Japan, producing civil war in the islands and requiring us to intern and support an enormous population" ("Now a Japanese 'Peril' in Hawaii," 1925, p. 13).

be justified as doomed from the start. Snyder and Mitchell (2006) quote Zygmunt Bauman as writing that "racism proclaims that certain blemishes of a certain category of people cannot be removed or rectified—that they remain beyond the boundaries of reforming practices, and will do so for ever" (p. 110).

A central aspect, then, of the object metaphor relates to individual and group identity and brings up a host of issues pertaining to imposed identities. According to William Brennan (1995), "In this process of objectification people are reduced to the level of insignificant matter that can be used, moved, manipulated, and disposed of with impunity" (p. 13). Gambrill (2012) added that those "who have the power to name and frame" others also have "the power to affect how what is framed and named is treated" (p. 128). The other becomes, in other words, the property or pawn of those who direct the labeling process. Because the ability to exert control and even ownership are both closely related to the capacity to identify, label, or diagnose the other, the desire to break away from this identification by others has been a primary factor in virtually all human rights movements. More important, as Freire (1970) noted in *Pedagogy of the Oppressed,* this objectification of the controlled group necessitates objectification of the identifiers themselves, whose higher lot in life becomes their own master status, regulating their social behavior and value orientation and thus limiting their own choices and capabilities.

Bosmajian (1983) contended that even people's very survival may depend on the label they are (or are not) given. Although one may automatically think of the more radical examples in this regard, such as Nazi labeling, there are certainly more contemporary, prosaic, and relevant ones. In the era of managed care, medical and mental health labeling often results in access to treatment, which certainly can have life-sustaining effects. It would be somewhat naïve, moreover, to assume that such labeling and classification is not at times "based on political, economic, and social grounds rather than on scientific" or humane ones (Gambrill, 2012, p. 129).

Devalued Individuals as Products

At times, devalued individuals and groups may be objectified by being compared to poorly made or substandard products. Some of those who supported expanding the inspection of immigrants during the early decades of the 20th century, for example, viewed these physical and mental examinations as a form of quality control similar to what one might implement in an automobile factory (Kraut, 1994). A pervasive view of immigrants at the time was that they were interchangeable tools of industry. Welcomed when low-wage work was needed for projects such as the railroads, their utility became marginal when such projects were completed, and they were seen as little more than excess inventory. Similarly, especially in a disposable culture such as the United States, elderly people too may be devalued as being past their prime, run down, outdated, or obsolete. Because productivity is such an important value in U.S. culture, people who are perceived as being nonproductive are at risk of having their status diminished.

Actuarialism, Utilitarianism, and Public Investment

Object metaphors are frequently evidenced by an actuarial view of humans, with particular people judged as being benefits or costs to society. Utilitarianism has been popularized in recent years by the controversial philosopher Peter Singer, whom I briefly discussed earlier as a founder of the animal rights movement. Utilitarianism carries with it an element of actuariality because one of its central themes is the greatest good for the greatest number. The argument is that one cannot feasibly give everything to everyone, so hard choices have to be made (Singer, 1994). This obviously means that certain needs (and thus, potentially, a person's having these needs) are valued over others. The late Paul Longmore (2003), a long-time disability advocate, cited Richard Lamm, the former governor of Colorado, as opposing educational spending for children with severe disabilities on the basis of the belief that this was a poor investment of taxpayer money.[15] This is obviously an extremely important issue for those working in social services because justifying what social services do on the basis of the public presumption of what constitutes a wise investment of public funds, or the implicit worth of certain client groups, is often an uphill battle.[16]

---

[15] Lamm used an especially interesting object metaphor in describing elderly individuals and their duty to die rather than force society to spend extensive resources trying to keep them alive past their appointed time. He said (as cited in Jecker, 2014) that "people who die without having life artificially extended are similar to 'leaves falling off a tree and forming humus for the other plants to grow up'" (para. 2).

[16] As with many other forms of dehumanization, the Nazis set the standard for viewing devalued groups as deficits or costs to society. They actually developed math assignments to be given to children in school that asked, for example, how many homes for middle-class families could be provided if a certain number of people with mental illness or mental retardation were not supported by the state (Weindling, 1989). Perhaps the most perverse example of this form of

Objectification also occurs in the social services field in response to agency public relations requirements. A limitless supply of funding for services cannot be assumed, and legislators are particularly loathe to suggest tax increases in the current economic and political climate. Many public agencies, in fact, are being starved of public funding and need to solicit support from other sources or the public. This means that social service agencies are forced to engage in greater efforts to secure funding and stand out among the service throng. These efforts, introduced in the previous chapter in the discussion of typifications, often tie into objectification, and particular clients, success stories, or examples of tragedies that could have been prevented are put forth as indicative of an entire client group or social problem that the agency is engaged in preventing. Perhaps the most controversial example of this has been the backlash by disability rights groups against "Jerry's Kids" and similar uses of poster children (Bennetts, 1993; Smit, 2003).[17] Again, social service agencies are often forced to make tough choices between the perceived exploitation of their clients and drawing on these exemplars as the most apt way to demonstrate the importance and benefit to the agency.

Medical Metaphor

The object metaphor closely relates to the medical metaphor, wherein diagnosis of the individual leads to a condition that becomes, at least in the eyes of members of the medical profession, the central identifier of the person. As Foucault (1965), Szasz (1970), Goffman (1961), and others have described in their writings, a core element of the object metaphor as it plays itself out in medicine, social work, or psychiatry is the power or status relationship between the physician, psychiatrist, or social worker and the patient, a relationship that is substantively reinforced by the diagnostic expertise that is granted to medical professionals. As these authors noted, good patients are in large part considered to be those who, without complaining, take on the role of the passive, unquestioning, grateful patient, thus covertly agreeing to their own objectification.

---

objectification by the Nazis was their bargaining with Jewish relief groups for the lives of Jews because Nazi functionaries would trade these lives for money, jewels, trucks, and so forth.

[17] To say that the late Jerry Lewis was a divisive figure in the disability community would be an understatement. Although many praised his efforts to raise money and awareness, others criticized him for objectifying his kids and awfulizing the impact of disability. His 1990 article in *Parade Magazine* ("If I Had Muscular Dystrophy") is an example of the pity perspective that fed the backlash to the telethons.

As alluded to previously, not only are individuals and presumably homogeneous groups objectified, but so too are those stigmatized places where they reside. Asylums and institutions, ghettoes, reservations, ethnic enclaves, nursing homes, and other spatial or geographic spaces may be subject to objectification. As Foucault (1965) noted, the use of abandoned leprosariums and almshouses as mental institutions seemed appropriate in large part because these spaces themselves had become so stigmatized that they could only appropriately serve another stigmatized class of people. "The nineteenth century," he wrote, would "insist that to the mad and to them alone be transferred these lands on which, a hundred and fifty years before, men had sought to pen the poor, the vagabond, the unemployed" (p. 57).

Many areas of social work obviously either operate in conjunction with medicine and medical professionals or have borrowed terminology, and thus metaphoric concepts, from medicine. As Beckett (2003) noted, "medicine has been a major source" of both the "official and colloquial language of social workers" (p. 632). It is especially important that those who work in medically related social work areas understand the variety of ways in which metaphoric descriptions can circumscribe conditions or treatments in a way that limits alternate ways of viewing them and thus stifles potentially creative approaches that may not be conducive to the prevailing metaphoric framing. Although labeling can feed objectification and have other ill effects, it is also obviously necessary to gain reimbursement for treatment. In their book *Dangerous Diagnostics,* Nelkin and Tancredi (1989) discussed many of the potential consequences that may arise with medical and other forms of diagnostics (also see Kirk & Kutchins, 1992).

OBJECTIFICATION, POSITIVE METAPHORS, AND DOUBLE BINDS

One might believe that a means of dealing with pejorative linguistic or conceptual metaphors would be to replace them with more positive options. I should note, however, that even what might be viewed as positive framings of groups also serve to foster stereotypical views and therefore do not necessarily provide a beneficial alternative to negative framings. A pertinent example of this is the model minority view of Asian Americans (Quinsaat, 2014). Central to this image is the assumption that

Asian Americans are economically and educationally successful, cause few problems within the social system (for example, crime), are generally unwilling to accept public assistance, and readily assimilate into American culture. Viewing such citizens from an actuarial standpoint, which again is central to the object metaphor, one might say they are net assets to the general public, providing more to society than they take. Even though this image is ostensibly positive, it supports a stereotype. This stereotype, moreover, could easily be used for the purpose of depreciating its targets. In other words, an Asian American youth who works hard and struggles to complete college may be given little personal credit for this accomplishment if others believe that she or he has the inherent or cultural wherewithal to succeed. In a sense, the targets of such a framing find themselves in a no-win situation because failure may be viewed as a personal outcome whereas success is in the genes.

One can think of a number of other such examples. The good wife and mother image of the 1950s was on its face positive (at least at the time), but it had very dark and patronizing undertones to it that have become more clear as time has progressed. Similarly, Adolf Hitler lionized the Aryan female and portrayed her (so long as she bore children for the Reich) as the female version of a soldier, essential to the health of the nation. Both the male as soldier and female as creator of future soldiers were utilitarian concepts, wherein the individual and his or her desires, needs, attributes, and unique qualities were subsumed by the need of the collective (Bock, 1983; Hillel & Henry, 1976). These examples also tie into objectification because they support the mechanistic metaphor, or the belief that a properly functioning system (family, community, workplace, nation) exists when, like a watch, every part performs its proper role in conjunction with the others.

Double Binds and Social Oppression

Both of the preceding examples of what were viewed as positive metaphors (model minority and the good wife and mother) relate to the double bind that implicitly props up many stereotypes and frequently supports oppression. Double binds, moreover, are often accompanied by metaphors. The term "double bind" is frequently used in social work to describe clients, social workers themselves, or others who find themselves in an untenable dilemma in which their decisions are strictly limited and either of their options may result in negative consequences. The woman who is involved in a violent relationship may be harmed by remaining in the relationship, but she could also lose her children to her abuser (at least for periods of time) or believe she will exacerbate the violence by sharing her situation or attempting to leave. A current example of a double bind in which clinicians often find themselves occurs when they must diagnose a client or one member of a couple to be reimbursed by an insurance provider (Crews & Hill, 2005).

In a broad macro sense, double binds often ensure that the members of marginalized groups submit to their objectification, especially by limiting their response options. One of the laudable aspects of Martin Luther King Jr.'s response to injustice relates to the fact that he realized that, in the South especially, where many African Americans felt the need to respond violently to the blatant discrimination and injustice they faced, this response would only serve to provide justification for this treatment. Such a response would play into and augment the stereotypical view that African Americans, and male African American in particular, were angry, emotional, and prone to violence. If they inspired fear, this would be highlighted and used to support their segregation and subjugation. King turned this stereotype on its head when, through nonviolent protest, he forced the existing white power structure to respond violently. For many, the image of the civil rights movement became not the angry African American man but rather the angry white man, symbolized by Bull Connor and George Wallace (Berger, 2011). Many Americans came to associate themselves with the protesters and support the movement because they felt a greater kinship to them than to their aggressors.

Other examples of double binds in which vulnerable groups have historically been placed include a California policy that disallowed Japanese immigrants from owning land and public boycotts of Jewish-owned businesses in New York. Both examples occurred early in the 20th century, and both related to similar fears that the population in question was attaining too much power, with the Japanese cornering the market on certain crops and Jews taking over clothing and related industries. Target groups may use subterfuge to skirt these policies (Japanese having Americans as shill buyers for their property, and Jews Americanizing their names or having their businesses in the name of a partner or other). In such cases, they could be accused of being duplicitous and underhanded, which served to support the existing stereotypes of Japanese and Jews as cunning, untrustworthy, and deceitful (Metrick-Chen, 2012).[18] Many additional examples can be found through which oppression and demeaning treatment are supported through double binds, and social policy frequently supports these efforts, often through covert mechanisms.

Labels, Diagnoses, and Metaphors in the Social Work Setting

Dehumanization stands as a primary mode of supporting oppression and repressive social policies. The beliefs that marginalized populations are animalistic, subhuman, or lower entities; that their value to society can be accurately gauged and weighted relative to others; and that the label they are given by diagnosticians tells one much about their individual essence are just a few of the ways in which people engage in depersonalizing and dehumanizing others. As such groups become increasingly dehumanized, their maltreatment becomes easier to justify, not only because they may seem to have less inherent value to society or their seeming inability to engage in rational thought moves them closer to animal status, but also out of pity, for who would want to live such a life?

It is important, I would argue crucial, that social workers engage with their clients (and others) in a true partnership. To the degree that it is possible, social workers must take pains to remove feelings of pity and differential status from their work with clients and to understand not only the benefits, but also the limitations of diagnostics and labeling (Gambrill, 2012; Kirk & Kutchins, 1992; Nelkin & Tancredi, 1989; Whitaker, 2002).

---

[18] The primary source literature contains many examples of each of these stereotypes. For anti-Jewish writing, the starting point is the series of re-publications titled *The International Jew* (1920). These four volumes are without question the most important anti-Semitic writings in the United States, and they fostered a strong anti-Jewish movement during the decade before the Third Reich. Henry Ford, although not the author of these publications, certainly funded them, and they originally appeared in the *Dearborn Independent*, a weekly publication owned by Ford. For the anti-Japanese, see, for example, Rowell (1913) or Steiner (1917).

5
Metaphors That Evoke Threat and Fear Responses

> *Wherever the Japanese have settled, their nests pollute the communities like the running sores of leprosy. They exist like the yellowed, smoldering discarded butts in an over-full ashtray, vilifying the air with their loathsome smells, filling all who have the misfortune to look upon them with a wholesome disgust and a desire to wash.*
> —*American Defender* magazine
> (as cited in McWilliams, 1935, p. 735)

> *The American people are sick of the yearly influx of hundreds of thousands of unassimilable aliens that pour in on them each year from every section of the world under the present laws. They feel the poison working in the veins of America[,] a slower poison than that which preceded the Three Per Cent Law, but a poison no less certain.*
> —K. Roberts (1924, p. 59)

Although linguistic and conceptual metaphors that serve to dehumanize and objectify marginalized populations are frequently used to restrict the rights of or foster stigma surrounding such people, another important mode of denigrating them is through the use of metaphors that support the belief that devalued groups pose an imminent threat to the wider community.[1] Metaphoric images and rhetoric that are frequently used to support fearmongering include the perception that the out-group is at war with society or is criminalistic and that their impact is potentially destructive to others, similar to a natural catastrophe or other large-scale

---
[1]Some portions of this chapter were previously published in O'Brien (2009).

calamity. Another fear-based theme is that such people constitute a point of potential metaphoric contagion and are a source of corruption that may well inject contaminants into and eventually cause the gradual but unremitting decay of the community or social body (O'Brien, 2018).

As with the examples provided in chapter 4, the various forms of adverse metaphors have much overlap, and many metaphor themes gain their strength from both dehumanizing their targets and at the same time presenting them as objects of fear. Certainly animalistic portrayals, for example, are often invoked because they both dehumanize and elicit fear. To reiterate, though, metaphors are largely contextual, and in some cases even fearful animalistic images or rhetoric have been used as positive analogues. Especially in wartime, nations may use such images to symbolize the strength of their fighting forces, as with Nazi Germany's use of the lion and wolf, described in chapter 4 (Sax, 2000). That being said, some destructive animals, such as the lowly rat, virtually always serve as an unfavorable point of comparison.

Images that solicit fear in particular evoke a primitive or instinctive response from people. Humans, like most animals, have an inborn need to protect themselves and their loved ones from perceived threats. This fear of real threats lends support for the potency of metaphoric ones. Fear-based rhetoric has always been effective in the domain of social policy in large part because politicians and other political stakeholders understand its influence. Come election time, people know they will be swamped with images of opposition politicians who are depicted as coddling terrorists, child molesters, criminals, atheistic communists, and illegal immigrants and as supporting or bowing down to whichever dictator or ruler happens to stand in as the Hitler of the day.[2] To quote Corey Robin (2004), "We have paid a terrible price for our flirtation with political fear, dishonoring its victims and disabling ourselves. Perhaps this is a good time to consider whether that price has been worth it" (p. 24).

As alluded to earlier, because fear is such a pervasive element of both people's social world and the political system, it has an extraordinarily important impact on social workers' clients as well as on the profession itself and how social workers are viewed. Many helping professionals

---

[2] Perhaps the most well-known (and potentially effective) such image was the Willie Horton commercial used by the George H. W. Bush campaign. This racially tinged commercial presented Democratic candidate Michael Dukakis as soft on crime, allowing dangerous (read: young and African American) criminals to walk the streets.

are engaged on a daily basis with people who instill fear (often covertly) into the wider community, whether this fear is related to crime, public health concerns (HIV), economic anxiety (people receiving government assistance), mortality fears (elderly individuals), or subconscious threats to bodily (people with disabilities) or mental integrity (people with diagnosed mental illnesses). Again, one of the reasons why social workers and other allies for social justice are often devalued in society is because they operate in liminal spaces that are identified by people who elicit fear in the general public, and they thus serve as a potential vector of contagion.

WAR AND OTHER FEAR-BASED METAPHORS

The war metaphor is characterized by the extensive deployment of military rhetoric or a general framing of a devalued group as an imminent threat to the nation's or community's well-being; therefore, the restriction of their rights is said to be warranted by the need to safeguard innocent people. Those who use such metaphors often contend that although measures of control or restriction are generally undesirable, especially in a nation that values personal freedom, such policies are at times necessary because of the nature of the threat at hand. The war metaphor is also a means of highlighting the contention that, although many problems and issues face the nation at any given time, a particular concern is preeminent and must be faced immediately and forcefully (Semino, 2008). Those invoking this metaphor position themselves as resolute protectors of the community. Groups and individuals who support legislative proposals that limit gay rights, for example, are quick to position themselves as defenders of the American family and traditional Judeo-Christian values rather than as mean-spirited dogmatists who oppose diversity, individual rights, and alternative worldviews. They also foster the perception that their efforts constitute a form of necessary self-defense against an aggressor.

The movement of people across geographic boundaries, the takeover of land or city property, the mass movement of a group into a job sector, and other types of territorial battles are frequently an important aspect of the war metaphor. A series of time-lapse maps, for example, that purports to show the disconcerting increase in the presence of a minority group in a neighborhood or region (usually symbolized by foreboding black coloring, which is especially likely to touch a chord with readers when the fear is an increase in the African American population or another population of color[3]) is one example of this. The target group is presented as being much like a foreign enemy, expanding its foothold in the nation and softening the ground for the presumptive oncoming horde of compatriots who will follow in their wake.

An us-against-them imperative arises with the war metaphor, and everyone is forced to take a side. Often, an ever-expanding litany of non-normative behaviors and beliefs may be subsumed under pejorative identifiers such as "disloyal," "criminalistic," "socialist," or "feeble-minded," and those who refuse to embrace such vague classifications may themselves be suspect. Because they cross borders, are of foreign origin, and may have largely unknown historical biographies and their loyalty to their new nation can be questioned for a time, incoming immigrants or refugees are particularly likely to be subject to the war metaphor, and thus large-scale immigration has frequently been considered to be an invasion (Steiner, 1917; Warne, 1913/1971). Those who argued in favor of restrictive immigration laws during the first decades of the 20th century said of immigrants that "like the hordes of old they are destined to conquer us in the end, unless by some miracle of human contriving we conquer them first" (Cannon, 1923, p. 330) and, they asked, was it was necessary that invaders "should come in warships instead of in the steerage hold of steam vessels before the migration can be called an invasion?" (Warne, 1913/1971, p. 2). Many similar examples of this exist, and one certainly does not have to search too long before coming across such rhetoric in the course of contemporary debates related to immigrants or refugees (see, for example, Chomsky, 2014; Cunningham-Parmeter, 2011; J. Lederer, 2013; Santa Ana, 2002). Those who support immigrants or refugees are often placed in an impossible situation, made to ensure that every immigrant of a particular group is safe. If this Herculean task cannot be accomplished, it is better to restrict the entire population to safeguard the community.[4]

---

[3] As one might expect, when the fear was Communist incursion, the coloring was apt to be blood red (Barson & Heller, 2001).

[4] In fact, after the attack on Pearl Harbor, all Japanese on the West Coast were interned, despite a lack of evidence that any were supporting the enemy. Those calling for their internment noted that this lack of known collusion was almost a sure sign that the Japanese in America were very well disciplined and would only attack en masse when the time was right. An Army colonel noted that the "fact that there has *not* been a single instance of disloyalty [on the part of Japanese on the Coast] can be a most ominous thing" (Bendetsen, 1942, p. 541). Again, this is an inescapable double bind.

War-Based Metaphors and Recent Public Policy

Requirements such as those in Arizona whereby immigrants (and citizens who may be perceived to be immigrants) need to carry and produce papers to prove their identity certainly closely resemble wartime demands for similar forms of identification that have been imposed on questionable subpopulations in the name of community protection. Again, war-related fears and immigrant invasions have close parallels. Bureaucratic requirements instituted in the name of community protection often serve as ways to mark the other as different or stigmatized and, as with the Jim Crow laws, additionally force target group members to embrace the identity that is imposed on them (Hale, 1998). Most periods characterized by wide-scale oppression have included the need for certain types of marking, branding, or self-identification, ostensibly for reasonable purposes: to protect the public (O'Brien, 2018). Again, this branding is often supported by altruistic arguments that the innocent members of such groups (for example, immigrants with the proper paperwork) can prove their innocence and not be mistakenly harmed. Vulnerable minority populations tend to be rightly fearful of having to carry papers or otherwise prove their innocence, for a number of reasons that are easy to guess, but mainly because this act is often a signal of more repressive policies to follow.

More important, in the age of terrorist fears (to a degree valid, certainly), it is somewhat difficult to tell what type of war this actually is, whether it will ever end, and how traditional war-related social control measures may be properly and ethically instituted. Although these issues are pressing, and the source of much debate, they are beyond the scope of this book. It is, however, important to note that both war and crime as well as public health fears have at times been exploited to serve particular corporate, political, media, or other powerful interests, with a degree of social control frequently being an outgrowth of this. A particular example that is relevant to social work interests pertains to anti-Communist fears and their subsequent detrimental impact on those areas of social service that can be interpreted as falling under the umbrella of socialism. To quote Fisher (1994), "the Red Scare and the return to normalcy [end of World War I] of the decade after 1919 destroyed many liberal and radical programs" (p. 29). Those programs that survived were required to embrace patriotism and refrain from any form of social service provision that could be construed as being in any way socialist. As Kim Nielsen

(2001) wrote, Helen Keller was forced to keep quiet about her own radical beliefs because broad knowledge of them would have diminished her ability to raise both awareness and funding for issues related to people with sensory disabilities. Certainly support in the United States for repeated efforts to develop a single-payer health care system has been adversely affected by labeling these plans as socialized medicine.

Crime Metaphors

Images and terminology that present the target group as criminalistic or terroristic constitute variants of the war metaphor. In some cases, they are more apt to be used as invective because criminals and terrorists are in some ways even more despicable than enemy soldiers. The former are more likely to attack innocent people and act in stealth, cowardly planning and conniving behind people's backs because they realize they cannot win a fair fight. They do not wear a uniform and they attempt to blend into society; therefore, they are attacking from within. Some of these images of the home-grown enemy are of people so cowardly that they will not fight at all, even in a sneaky, underhanded way. Like the Communists of the 1930s and 1950s or, more recently, gays and atheists, these groups are said to be intent on covertly brainwashing impressionable youths whom they intend to do their dirty work and destroy the nation from within (Church League of America/Edgar Bundy Ministries, 1961; Dannemeyer, 1989; McCarthy, 1952).

In some cases, the target group's instinctual or hereditary criminal propensity is believed to be so certain and so beyond their control that preventive measures can be taken against the target group even before they engage in any criminal behavior. Cesare Lombroso, the 19th-century Italian criminologist discussed in chapter 4, contended that people with epilepsy were so incapable of controlling their behaviors that they should be institutionalized as a preventive public safety measure even before committing any crime (Lombroso, 1968; Maudsley, 1898).[5] In other cases, threatening subgroups may be diagnosed with a mental illness so they can be removed from society to protect both themselves and the public. In his book *The Protest Psychosis,* Jonathan Metzl (2009) described

---

[5]Similarly, a number of states developed very loose institutionalization laws during the eugenics era so that individuals who were determined to be feebleminded could easily be forcibly institutionalized. Of course, the crime that was presumed to have been prevented in these cases was a socially toxic form of procreation (J. D. Smith, 1985; Trent, 1994).

this in relation to male African Americans in the 1960s. Public fear of riots and groups such as the Black Panthers was such that many male African Americans who had been accused of even minor crimes were often deemed schizophrenic, in which case they could be placed in an institution even if the demonstrations in which they engaged did not constitute criminal activity. In his various books, Thomas Szasz (1963, 1970) often discussed the use of the mental health system to support social and political control efforts.

The requirement that social workers and other allies for social justice serve as social control agents has been a matter of controversy since virtually the beginning of the profession. The line between assisting people to access necessary services and acting as an agent of the state or breaching confidentiality, often through communications with law enforcement personnel, employers, parents, or other authority figures, can be very hard to adequately discern. Regardless of how it is framed, in the eyes of many segments of the public, and particularly many marginalized populations, social service workers are frequently viewed as informers and professionals who support allegiance to the existing status quo, which has been designed by and serves the interests of those in power (D. Roberts, 2002).

Natural Catastrophe Metaphors

Similar to the war metaphor, the natural catastrophe metaphor portrays the group in question as analogous to a potentially cataclysmic act of nature, such as a flood, fire, tornado, earthquake, or, especially when people of Asian descent are the targets of control, a tsunami or typhoon ("The Typhoon," 1912). The most conspicuous example of this is the extensive use of flood rhetoric in describing immigrants, both past and present. One supporter of immigration control argued, for example, that if strict limitations were not enforced, "the flood gates will be down and a turgid sea of aliens will inundate our seaports" ("Guarding the Gates," 1924, p. 401). As with most other uses of the natural catastrophe metaphor, the flood image is used in part because it aptly symbolizes the issue at hand, because immigrants generally travel over the water (O'Brien, 2003a) and are seen as inundating territory and making it unfit for civilized habitation. Floods (as well as other major natural catastrophes) also often bring disease and contagion in their wake, and thus their impact may be widespread and continue to negatively affect even groups that are not directly in their paths.[6] Like blood (more on this in the "Fears of Contagion and Degeneration" section), water is also diffuse and conjures images of quick and widespread contamination that cannot easily be contained.

PRESUMPTIVE RESPONSE TO FEAR-BASED METAPHORS

War, crime, and natural catastrophe metaphors predicate a harsh, draconian approach to the identified problem, just as the War on Drugs favors spending on imprisonment and interdiction over education and treatment. If those who use and sell illegal drugs are perceived as enemy combatants, a strategy built around treatment and education would hardly be an appropriate policy solution (Ellwood, 1995). One cannot treat terrorists or educate enemy soldiers and convince them to lay down their arms. The war metaphor also implies that a zero-sum approach to a particular social problem or issue is a reasonable means of viewing the situation. In other words, it separates various human factions into classes fighting over scarce resources, with no possibility of a middle ground. Voters are informed that any policies that are directed to help the group in question will harm themselves by invoking a simplistic redistribution schema. Frequently, especially when the group, because of its presumed laziness, selfishness, inherent incompetence, or other related reasons, is viewed as unworthy of aid, these zero-sum arguments are couched in Malthusian or social Darwinistic language. If the target group is assisted in its efforts to survive, propagandists note, this not only reinforces their indolence or incompetence, but also fosters an untenable birth differential between the nation's earners and users (Sidel, 2000). The threat that these groups pose to the rest of society, the argument continues, especially because of their increasing numbers, is not unlike the threat posed by a foreign enemy attempting to take over the nation.

The fear that surrounded the eugenics movement and the presumption that people with feeblemindedness and other degenerate groups were procreating in large numbers is closely connected to the more recent fear

---

[6]Conversely, water also purifies. As noted, one of the reasons Nazi gas chambers were disguised as showers was because they were seen as a form of purification. Similar to the term "racial cleansing," in this case it was the race that was being purified. Another example is given by Bauman (1997, p. 5), who noted Michel Foucault's description of the *Narrenschiffen,* or ship of fools. During the Middle Ages, one means of relieving a locality of its paupers and people with mental illness or other disabilities was by sending them away on a boat. The sea was perceived as a vehicle of purification, which such people presumably needed.

of mothers who receive public assistance purposefully having very large families to increase their support allotments. Between the 1930s and 1960s, involuntary sterilization, especially in southern states, evolved from focusing primarily on morons to targeting poor, usually African American women. This evolution was generally seamless because the two groups were thought to overlap considerably (Black, 2003; Washington, 2006).

These days, the government or private advocacy groups seem to launch a war on something (drugs, cancer, childhood obesity, illiteracy, and so forth) with some frequency. Although I certainly do not want to discount or minimize the degree of these problems, I should note that the war metaphor may give rise to numerous negative unintended consequences. As has frequently been pointed out, such depictions may serve to, unknowingly perhaps, place those who are identified as victims in the position of enemies of society (Sontag, 1990). Many have argued that the war on drugs has served to isolate, label, and criminalize addicts or even casual users. There is a very fine line, moreover, between declaring war on a social problem and declaring war against the people who are fighting or experiencing the problem. Richard Gwyn (1999) wrote that "the military metaphor provides us all . . . with an identifiable evil that is all too easily transferred onto the people who are subject to the illnesses themselves" (p. 207). Although get-tough policies may be emotionally satisfying, they may also drive problems underground because individuals may be fearful of seeking support at an early stage and therefore do not access preventive services.

When target groups are not seen as enemies, they are apt to be viewed as unfortunate victims who need to be saved, as people with disabilities are often framed. Susan Sontag (1990), in her writing on cancer and metaphor, noted that the meaning underlying the metaphors people assign to diseases may enhance the suffering of those who are diagnosed with such conditions and adversely affect their ability to cope with such conditions (also see Davis, 2002). Individual agency may be diminished, and these people presumably need the government, social service professionals, or others to come to their defense. Vallis and Inayatullah (2016) added that it "has almost become a truism that whenever there's a government campaign declaring war on something—whether it is drugs, terrorism or disease—one of the first casualties is civil liberties" (p. 5). Just as such liberties may be abrogated in an actual war in the name of supporting public safety, so too may they be abrogated when the war is only metaphoric.

ORGANISM METAPHOR

The organism metaphor is a means of describing the collective social body or nation as similar in many ways to a human body. Although the organism metaphor has been around for centuries in various guises (Herzogenrath, 2010), it became a principal means of viewing society and social problems in large part during the mid- to late 19th century. It was at this time that scientific research into the germ theory of disease was expanding public knowledge of how diseases spread, subsequently leading to massive public health and sanitation measures (J. Duffy, 1992; DuPuis, 2015; Musolff, 2004; Tomes, 1998). This focus on social purity is important for social work professionals because the profession matured in conjunction with the early public health movement, and many early social reformers viewed their work as a form of community hygiene.

Disease in Organism Metaphors

The health and well-being of the community or national organism requires that all of its components work together efficiently toward common goals and to nurture the body of the collective (Levine, 1995; O'Brien, 1999, 2018). As would others, Herbert Spencer (1904) compared the unimportant or diseased members of the community to parts of the human body that were unnecessary or cancerous and that required treatment or removal. Similar to germs, bacteria, or viruses, target groups are often viewed as invasive or destructive social elements that are capable of infecting the mass of the community (DuPuis, 2015). Zygmunt Bauman wrote (1997) that "sweeping the floor and stigmatizing traitors or banishing strangers appear to stem from the same motive of the preservation of order, of making and keeping the environment understandable and hospitable to sensible action" (p. 8). Methods of segregation such as imprisonment, institutionalization, and the mandated use of separate facilities, therefore, are often presented as community protection measures, similar to other means of protecting public health. At times, such segregation measures may even carry a public health moniker and be described as a form of quarantine.

An obsession with germs, viruses, disease contagion, household and community cleanliness, and the protection of one's body quickly came to have vast metaphoric import during the first decades of the 20th century, and this has continued unabated. According to Tomes (1998), an etiquette manual from the late 19th century informed its female readers that "cleanliness is the outward sign of inward purity" (p. 62), as well as of upper-class status. This metaphor is especially potent because the intrusion of harmful or disgusting entities into one's body is among the most instinctive and powerful of fears.[7] Invasive microscopic creatures entering one's body and reproducing or growing once inside is the stuff of both nightmares and countless horror and science fiction movies.

The Alien and the Foreign in the Context of the Organism Metaphor

People fear the incorporation into their body of anything alien or foreign. This concern plays itself out metaphorically in their trepidation regarding inappropriate or potentially harmful foreign people in places where they do not belong, whether this is not-in-my-backyard fears of social service agencies or halfway houses setting up shop in an otherwise nice community or of a large number of minorities moving into white neighborhoods. As alluded to previously, there is a close analogy between protection of one's physical body from contamination and keeping the nation or social body safe from undesirable immigrant or other groups.[8]

Over the past few decades, many writings have delineated the importance of the organism metaphor (although it is often not referred to as such) in relation to restrictive immigration efforts (Markel & Stern, 2002; Santa Ana, 2002). This is nothing new; during the late 19th and early 20th centuries, immigration restriction was often connected to concepts of incorporation, digestion, contagion, poisoning, and so forth (O'Brien, 2003a, 2018). Just as the melting pot was the primary metaphor used to describe immigration, undesirable immigrants were often seen as unhealthy ingredients in the American recipe. A 1924 cartoon in *The Literary Digest* is indicative of this; it shows Uncle Sam sitting at a dinner table turning down a helping of Japanese immigration, saying that it would give him digestive trouble ("End of the 'Melting-Pot' Theory,"

---

[7] Although the presumptive connection between vaccines and autism was largely based on faulty research (Mnookin, 2011), for example, one might contend that a primary reason for the staying power of this belief is the high degree of concern people have over what they take into their bodies or, in this case, allow to be put into the bodies of their children.

[8] Karen Bancroft (2012), for example, noted that an effort in Tacoma, Washington, to keep people from going into prostitution zones had the title "Stay Out of Areas of Prostitution" (p. 71). One might assume that it is not entirely coincidental that the acronym for the policy was SOAP. Not only is cleansing one's body similar on a subconscious level to cleansing the community, but people have an inherent desire to physically cleanse themselves when they have been polluted, even if the taint was purely imagined.

1924, p. 15). More recently, national–physical body fears often pertain to illegal immigrants who are presumably bringing diseases into the nation. In his article "Contaminated Communities," J. David Cisneros (2008) described the numerous ways, many metaphoric, in which immigrants have been portrayed as pollutants or toxic entities (also see Cunningham-Parmeter, 2011; Park & Kemp, 2006; Santa Ana, 2002).

Disease as Foreign and the Social Impact

It is interesting, although not at all surprising, that those diseases that appear to arise from either a foreign source or a devalued subgroup solicit particular contempt (Harper & Raman, 2008; S. C. Miller, 1969; Nelkin & Gilman, 1988). The general public both feels somewhat protected from such conditions, as long as real or imagined boundaries are maintained, and at the same time often fears such diseases out of proportion to the damage they actually invite.[9]

Similarly, Soffer and Ajzenstadt (2010) wrote that particular disease conditions (as well as the people who harbor them) are more apt to be given a foreign identity if the condition or diagnosis itself is highly contagious, heavily stigmatized, or both. They described HIV as a disease that inevitably comes from elsewhere. Although their research focused on Israeli views of HIV, there is certainly a close similarity to how the condition was viewed in the United States, especially early in its evolution. Soffer and Ajzenstadt compared HIV with heart disease. They contended that because the latter is not contagious and is usually associated with nonstigmatized groups, it is not perceived as having a foreign origin, nor does it solicit the profound sense of dread that HIV does. Thomas Yingling (as cited in Bennett, 2009) noted that "American feeling for the body inscribes disease as foreign and allows AIDS to be read therefore as anti-American" (p. 94).[10] In her classic *Illness as Metaphor and AIDS and Its Metaphors,* Sontag (1990) noted that AIDS, like swine fever and

---

[9]Consider, for example, influenza as opposed to the Ebola virus. The former has been around for centuries, and one could say people have become somewhat comfortable with it, even though it kills thousands of Americans every year. Ebola, however, caused a near panic in the country, even though it led to only a few deaths (see Goodwin & Chemerinsky, 2016).

[10]Vallis and Inayatullah (2016) noted that during the tuberculosis epidemic early in the 20th century, advertisements for public health products "personified germs as characters of African, Italian, Chinese, Slavic and Jewish descent" (p. 5). In his book *Racial Hygiene,* Proctor (1988) included a Nazi propaganda image with a microscope showing infectious germs, with the germs being the Star of David and the hammer and sickle of the Soviet Union (figure 34).

related diseases, elicited much fear not only because it was associated with devalued community groups, but also because of the belief that it originally arose from nonhuman animals. Thus the disease breached not only class and racial barriers, but also the boundary between species.

This conceptualization of disease as foreign does not only relate to the desire to protect national boundaries from penetration. In 1908, an article appearing in *McClure's Magazine* noted that

> seldom does a Southern State discover yellow fever within its own borders. It is always Mississippi that finds the infection in New Orleans, and Louisiana that finds it in Galveston. This apparently curious condition of affairs is explicable readily enough, on the ground that no State wishes to discover the germ in its own veins, but is quite willing . . . to point out the bacillus in the system of its neighbor. (S. H. Adams, 1908, pp. 247–248)

This gives rise to an important issue, especially for social workers who are engaged in public health efforts. When it comes to disease threats, risk assessment and the subsequent protective or public health measures that people support are seldom grounded in rational research or measures. People have a strong inherent aversion to disease, and thus their response is likely to be highly emotional. Add to that the fact that certain diseases are highly stigmatized not only because of their impact, but also because of how they are perceived (for example, as being a disease of marginal or poor populations or being transmitted through immoral routes). Such stigmatization can have numerous detrimental effects vis-à-vis public health efforts.

First, people may continue to engage in extremely unhealthy habits (for example, smoking) while at the same time taking pains to refrain from personal contact in situations in which it would be extraordinarily unlikely (a person with HIV) or even impossible (someone with a seizure disorder) that they would become infected. Second, heavy stigma may lead people to refuse to be honest about conditions, which mitigates efforts to engage in disease surveillance and transmission control. According to Goodwin and Chemerinsky (2016), for example, early in the 20th century smallpox was often "unreported among whites because of 'the shame they felt being caught with'" (p. 963) what was considered to be a disease of African Americans. As seen with HIV, this stigma is sometimes so heavy it will even follow people to the grave; many obituaries of those who have died from AIDS have purposefully been silent about the cause of death or other indicators of the disease (for example, not mentioning a partner in the list of surviving relatives).

Fears of Contagion and Degeneration

Concerns regarding contagion are particularly apparent in the history of race relations. This can be seen, for example, in some of the Jim Crow laws. In testimony before Congress during deliberations on the Civil Rights Act, Attorney General Robert F. Kennedy noted that in Greenwood, South Carolina, the city code made it "unlawful for any person operating a cafe, restaurant, or drinking fountain to serve colored people and white people with the same dishes and glasses" ("Civil Rights-Public Accommodations," 1963, p. 20), even after they had been washed. A similar contagion fear led to the segregation of blood by race when transfusions were first developed, as well as policies against cross-racial organ transplantation (S. E. Lederer, 2008). Certainly one unintended consequence of the former example is that numerous soldiers fighting in World War II and the Korean War died because race-suitable blood or organs were not available. As one might assume, blood takes on a particularly important role in racial and other forms of spread, especially related to fears of miscegenation, and its potency can be gauged by the one-drop rule: Only a very small amount of foreign blood was enough to taint someone and secure their identity as a stigmatized person.[11]

The literature also shows that anti-Communism was often described using organism and disease metaphors (Charteris-Black, 2009; Gregg, 2004; Lawrence, 1960). Ambassador George Kennan wrote in 1953 that the

> germ of Communist oversimplification rode like a malignant bacilus [sic] . . . in the veins of Western society, powerless to disrupt the functioning of the organism so long as health and

---

[11] During the Nazi era, the Germans gave blood an even higher degree of potency. Some German race hygienists argued that once an Aryan woman had intercourse with (or, in the language of the Nazis, was raped by) a Jew, she could never again bear an Aryan child, even if the father was a pure Aryan. Fritz Fink, a German writer, said that such a woman would be lost to her people forever (cited in Biale, 2007, p. 139; also see Thurston, 1935, p. 101). This and the one-drop rule are similar to what Beck (2011) referred to as "dose insensitivity." Even minute doses of particular polluted substances are enough to have a widespread adverse impact. An example he gave is that of a container of juice in which a roach has been dipped. Even if the container is huge, and the juice filtered, many people would likely still refuse to drink it (pp. 22–23).

vigor were present, but ready to seize on the slightest ulterior weakness in order to poison, to disintegrate, and to kill. (p. 10)

For propagandists, a side benefit of the use of the organism metaphor is that it can send a powerful, though often covert, message that the group in question must be isolated, lest others, especially those with a predisposition to the metaphoric disease in question, become suspected carriers. As with the anti-Communist periods, individuals who interact with target group members may become contaminated, and this circle of contagion can grow ever wider:

> Careful watch must be kept over people who call themselves liberals, for a liberal is really a Communist in disguise. The foreign-born and the Negroes also bear watching—the foreign-born because they undoubtedly have brought some revolutionary and un-American ideas with them to this country and the Negroes because the Communists plan to use them as the shock troops of the revolution. (Strong, 1941, p. 151)

As noted in chapter 4, an important use of the organism metaphor for social work purposes is parasitic terminology, especially to describe people receiving government benefits (Vallis & Inayatullah, 2016). Many scholars have noted that the targets of dehumanizing rhetoric are often compared to particularly loathsome and repulsive animals, such as parasites, lice, termites, bugs, and other vermin (Brennan, 1995; Keen, 1986; Levin, 1971; Lowenthal & Guterman, 1949/1970). These animals are not only harmful but inconsequential. As noted previously, killing lice or bugs is altogether different from killing large animals, even ones that may appear threatening. People do not perceive such animals as having independent personalities, and their destruction does not have to be justified or rationalized because it is viewed as necessary for the purposes of community health. Actual or metaphoric depictions of such animals symbolize waste and degeneration, the eating away of that which is healthy and good. As Sam Keen (1986) wrote, "The lower down in the animal phyla the images descend, the greater sanction is given to the soldier [or social control agent] to become a mere exterminator of pests" (p. 61). These parasitic metaphors gradate into medical metaphors as the organisms become ever smaller and inconsequential—becoming, in the end, germs, viruses, and cancer cells (O'Brien, 1999, 2018).

Another important facet of the organism metaphor as it relates to social service professionals and others who might be involved in community organizing or development is that certain features of a community or neighborhood may be depicted through the lens of the contagion–disease theme. Urban enclaves, especially poor ones, may be described as centers of metaphoric contamination and toxicity whose growth threatens outlying communities, not unlike an expanding cancer taking over healthy tissue. Discussing the immigration restriction era, Park and Kemp (2006) wrote that immigrant neighborhoods were described by early social workers and other urban planners "as malignant growths from which a host of ills flowed" (p. 721). Cisneros (2008) and Sibley (1995) have provided more recent descriptions of immigrant communities as sources of pollution. Gentrification and other programs that redevelop decaying areas may be viewed as a form of sanitation (Todolí, 2007). The deconcentration of poverty[12] "is based on a disease model of poverty in which the poor themselves are the agents of infection" and its goal is "to excise and dismember a tumor, to flush the site of disease" (Greenbaum, Hathaway, Rodriguez, Spalding, & Ward, 2008, p. 223).

Reification of the Organism Metaphor

As noted in chapter 1, metaphors can be reified, or made to appear real, through certain political or societal actions or policies. The overlay of pollution and space provides a good example of this. People who are viewed as devalued or as potential metaphoric contagion vectors are often relegated either to stigmatized institutional environments or to what Sibley (1995) referred to as "residual spaces."[13] These spaces are apt to become disease inducing, and their residents therefore become contagious in a real sense, providing further justification for their segregation.[14] Speaking of Europe,

---

[12]For those unfamiliar with the concept, poverty deconcentration involves widely dispersing those who live in the poorest neighborhoods throughout a broader area (for example, through Section 8 housing vouchers) under the assumption that this will benefit the uprooted residents in a number of ways.

[13]Again the term "marginalized" is appropriate because such people may literally be moved to the far margins or borders of (or beyond) society. During the institutionalization era, for example, insane asylums and later facilities for people with epilepsy and feeblemindedness were normally constructed beyond the boundaries of the community (Trent, 1994).

[14]W. I. Miller (1997) described the interconnection among spatial separation, contagion threats, and social class. He noted that in general those with greater wealth and of higher class have larger properties. Although one might assume the primary reason for this is to flaunt their high status or create a more personal space, he contended that a side benefit to large boundaries is that they serve to protect such people from possible pollution (metaphoric as well as actual) from others.

Sibley wrote that the "fear of 'polluting Gypsies' leads to attempts by the dominant society to consign them to unsanitary residual spaces where the stereotypical associations are confirmed" (p. 68). In one particularly egregious case, in the 1950s and 1960s the Willowbrook State School in New York purposefully infected clients with hepatitis to study the disease, rationalizing that the disease was so endemic in the facility that patients were likely going to contract it anyway (Rothman, 1982). This was only one in a long series of efforts to use devalued people as test subjects to study various forms of contagion (Washington, 2006). As noted in chapter 4, Foucault and other writers have noted that stigmatized people are often relegated to environments that have previously been inhabited by other stigmatized groups. This juxtaposition solidifies both their objectification and the perception that they serve as a likely source of pollution.

Again, I return to the argument that both metaphoric and real contagion fears are closely related to people's sense of disgust and repugnance (W. I. Miller, 1997; Rozin et al., 2009). This has great pertinence to social workers who engage with individuals who either live in what are considered to be disease-inducing geographic or institutional spaces or who are perceived to be diseased entities. Miller (1997) contended that disgust plays an important role in the maintenance of societal hierarchies and class-based categorization and that "it behooves social and political theory to care about these emotions and how they structure" (p. 18) and help to maintain such hierarchies.

Pizarro and Inbar (2015) described a variety of empirical studies that seem to demonstrate the relationship between disgust and contagion fears and social or political decision making. As they noted, individuals with high disgust sensitivity are more likely to be repelled by or render harsh moral judgments regarding certain social behaviors. Because by their nature sexual activities are obviously closely connected to the threat of contagion, this connection is particularly strong in relation to issues such as homosexuality, non-normative gender identities or forms of sexual expression, and prostitution.

Organism Metaphors and Perceived Threats

A good deal of overlap exists between the war and organism metaphors, especially because the two are intertwined in describing the battle that occurs between people's natural (immune system) or artificial (drugs, surgery) bodily defenses and invading diseases (Annas, 1995; Mayer &

Weingart, 2012; Reisfield & Wilson, 2004; Stein, 1995). In fact, no clear boundary exists between the two broad types. Certainly the most obvious example of this is the denigration of Jews in Nazi Germany. The German propaganda machine not only frequently described Jews as both violent criminals or an enemy force and an invading parasite or bacteria, but also often used such metaphors side by side (Keen, 1986; Proctor, 1988; Weindling, 2000). As noted earlier, both metaphors tend to reinforce one another, and they are largely interchangeable, especially because they may be used in the context of many areas of social service.

Fear is an emotion that is hard-wired into humans, and to a large degree people's inherent response to perceived threats has little connection to the realistic nature of the threat. Political stakeholders understand well the degree to which fearmongering can serve to frame an opposition campaign or candidate or provide a desired perspective on a particular issue or group. Social workers and allies for social justice issues should pay particular attention to metaphors that are based in fear or alarm. As alluded to previously, social workers often work with individuals who already elicit discomfort or anxiety, often for reasons not fully understood by those giving way to these feelings. The social problems faced by many client populations are incongruous with the just-world beliefs that many would like to maintain, and this is particularly true when children fall victim.

It is important that social work professionals understand that not only politicians but also media sources have a vested interest in certain presentations that instill fear or anger. These examples or stories then play an important role in how the social problem is viewed by the public. Social workers often find themselves in a contradictory position vis-à-vis this issue. On the one hand, destigmatization of client groups often requires a diminishment of the fear that may surround them, whereas, on the other, viewing the social problem as important often requires that it be conceptualized as a threat or that the most egregious examples of the problem be typified. Indeed, the war metaphor is inviting to social workers because it may lead not only to greater recognition of a social problem, but also to increased resources to fight it. As noted, though, social workers need to keep in mind that a battle against the problem often supports denigrating or paternalistic views of those who are affected by it.

6
Implications for Social Work Study, Practice, and Policy Advocacy

Most of what we understand in public discourse is not in the words themselves, but in the unconscious understanding that we bring to the words.
—Lakoff (2008, p. 43)

Mental fragments, dislodged from their historical and philosophical moorings but still poignant, capable of stirring up feelings, are waiting on the shelves for use at any appropriate time.
—Ewen and Ewen (2006, p. 491)

As the first two decades of the 21st century come to a close, there is a pervasive feeling among many citizens that democracy is, if not imperiled, at least in need of dramatic and immediate repair. It seems as though both politicians and voters are paying an ever-increasing amount of attention to the most superficial elements of social problems and the policies that relate to them. Citizens are awash in propaganda, spin, push polls, and even outright fabrications that masquerade as serious analysis. Bombast and name calling has taken the place of civil discussion, and few voters have the time or inclination to truly analyze policy or intellectually wade through the political morass that surrounds us. Citizens constantly question, and for good reason, whether their elected representatives would break ranks with their party or political action committee supporters if the good of the nation was at stake. Certainly some of these themes have a long history in American politics, but it does seem that all these concerns have moved into hyperdrive in recent years.

Unfortunately, marginalized groups frequently find themselves in the crosshairs of these developments. As people attempt to make sense of the free-floating anxiety they feel, politicians and other stakeholders provide ready explanations for why devalued groups are responsible for this uneasiness and fear. Scapegoats provide both a sense of comfort and a helpful distraction. The desire for social work students and those working in the field to engage in policy analysis to support social justice has long been a hallmark of the profession, but it has never been more important than it is today.

In this final chapter, I briefly take up what I see as the major implications of problem and policy metaphors as an expanding field of interest for both social work education and practice itself. Infusing metaphoric content is crucial in social work education because practitioners are most likely to become familiar with their need to understand metaphors through their own undergraduate or graduate studies; therefore, much of this final chapter focuses on ways of interjecting such content into social work curricula, and particularly into policy and social justice or diversity classes. There are, however, justifiable reasons to make metaphoric content a supplemental feature of virtually every aspect of the social work curriculum. Indeed, the more such content becomes integrated within an overall curriculum, the better students will be at understanding metaphoric content in the various areas of their lives. First, though, I briefly discuss one of the major ethical quandaries that arises from the issues described in this book, specifically related to the use of an alternative metaphor framing. I draw on the Patient Protection and Affordable Care Act (ACA) (2010) to provide a concrete example.

HEALTH CARE POLICY LANGUAGE: FREEDOM, RESPONSIBILITY, AND RIGHT

Often the most complicated policy areas are framed in the simplest of ways. One recent example is the ACA, also known as "Obamacare." A large portion of the public embraced opposing arguments surrounding individual freedom, and conservative critics of the bill gained ownership of the issue, at least among this sector of the voting public, by homing in on this specific concept. In fact, the proposed 2017 Republican version of the policy was titled the Patient Freedom Act (Gorin & Moniz, 2017). Freedom is among Americans' most cherished values, and metaphors related to freedom are frequently used in framing efforts. At first glance, the argument that all citizens should have the right to either purchase health insurance or not—that such purchase should be similar to that of any other commodity—seems quite reasonable.

Although hindsight is 20/20, it may be that those who support the movement toward universal health coverage in the United States missed the opportunity to find their own master metaphor by which the policy could be framed to counter freedom. One value that trumps freedom in many situations, and a value especially held by conservatives and libertarians, is individual responsibility. All people are expected to carry their own weight, and metaphors that relate to irresponsibility, such as the welfare recipient as parasite, have long been used to good effect by conservatives for the dual purpose of limiting expenditures and stigmatizing recipients.

People's freedoms are limited when those freedoms have an adverse impact on others. The best way to have politically countered the Republican framing of health care might have been to present those who did not carry health insurance as drags on society, because they could obviously have a major illness for which they would get treatment and, if unable to pay, would then be pushing these costs on to the more responsible citizens. In relation to health care, though, the freedom argument does not hold up, because people do not have the freedom to either get sick or not, nor do they realistically have the freedom to forgo costly major medical treatment necessary to prolong their life or greatly improve their quality of life. Although they may have such freedom theoretically, in the real world they will attempt to access care, regardless of the ability to pay.

I include this example for several reasons. First, as noted, policy options often boil down to the most basic of concepts and their accompanying metaphors (Lakoff, 1996, 2008). In the right to individual freedom and fears of socialized medicine, opponents of the ACA were able to develop nutshell talking points that spoke to a large cross-section of the public and connected with concerns about government overreach. Supporters of the ACA were unable to effectively counter these framings. Although the policy did pass, it was watered down in many ways and has faced continued opposition and efforts to replace it with a much weaker version or end it altogether. In addition, a number of its supporters became politically vulnerable because they voted for it. Many of the advocates' arguments constituted preaching to the choir and did not resonate strongly outside of supporters (for example, health care as a basic right or arguments centering on empathy), whereas the demand for individual responsibility, a conservative value, might have been more effective.

Certainly some groups have co-opted conservative responsibility arguments in support of progressive proposals. When the Americans with Disabilities Act of 1990 (ADA) was being debated in 1989, disability rights groups argued that increased workplace accommodations for people with disabilities would allow many to become taxpayers and decrease their dependence on government support. Of course, these advocates refrained from the more derogatory linguistic metaphors related to economic dependence, such as the parasite metaphor. Moreover, they contended that this dependence was forced on such people by a combination of lack of accommodations, harmful misconceptions of disability, and government policies that served as disincentives to gaining employment (Longmore, 2003; O'Brien & Ellegood, 2005). In the era of welfare reform, the need to support a policy that would allow those with disabilities to gain entry to the workplace was a mode of framing that spoke directly to conservative politicians who might otherwise have been wary of forcing restrictive regulations onto businesses.

Although framing health insurance and health care as a requirement of responsible citizenship rather than as a basic right might have resonated with conservatives, many social workers would no doubt have bristled at this suggestion. There are many reasons why people do not carry health insurance, and framing everyone without it as irresponsible and presumably self-serving seems overly harsh, stigmatizing, and simply inaccurate. Such a mode of framing also runs counter to the strengths perspective of social work, leading to one of the more interesting ethical quandaries related to the use of metaphors in social policy. As noted earlier, one might think that the best response to a particular framing of a problem or policy is simply to replace the metaphor. This is problematic, however, because metaphors tend to foster stereotyping. This is particularly true regarding the problems that social workers face, because such metaphors will generally devolve to a particular marginalized population.

For the sake of argument, though, suppose that the best political means of gathering broad-based support for the ACA and neutralizing arguments surrounding individual freedom was to focus extensively on responsibility (and thus irresponsibility). Do the political gains that might be wrought from framing the policy in a way that could forestall or at least lessen efforts to end it offset the negative characterization of many poor and middle-class people and families? This is an ethical dilemma that one is often faced with when considering alternative metaphoric framings. Lakoff (1996) has argued that conservatives have gained ownership of a number of social problems, and thus the policies that relate to them, because they have a much better awareness of how to effectively use rhetoric to meet their goals. However, pejorative metaphors and overt rhetorical manipulation, especially when based on fear, is anathema to many people. To repeat, even what could be considered at face value to be a positive metaphor, such as the model minority or supercrip, can under closer inspection have denigrating undertones that foster stigma.

As with the ADA example, however, one should consider ways of reframing the health care debate using responsibility rhetoric and arguments that coincide with the strengths perspective and do not support stigma. As Clark (1987) noted in her writings on sympathy, people are more likely to elicit sympathy and provide a greater sympathy margin to individuals who have characteristics in common with them or with whom they identify. Most people know individuals who have suffered, emotionally or economically, because of adverse aspects of the health care system. Encouraging these individuals to share their stories could affect problem framing. Moreover, freedom arguments need to be questioned if families, especially those who have a member with a pre-existing medical condition, cannot afford insurance. Although many conservative politicians contend that their proposed health care revisions will still allow access to health insurance for such people, they say little about the potential affordability of such plans. Arguments focusing on access and individual freedom are fairly meaningless if they exist only in theory.

IMPLICATIONS FOR SOCIAL WORK

The nature of policy practice as it exists within the profession and is taught in social work education programs will need to adapt to prepare professionals to effectively advocate in a constantly changing social and political landscape. An awareness of both linguistic and conceptual metaphors and the ability to deconstruct metaphoric language are crucial for social work educators, students, and practitioners for a wide variety of reasons, many of which have been delineated within the pages of this book. It seems that the more bizarre and inexplicable the social and political world becomes, the more people struggle to make sense of not only where they are and how they arrived here but, more important, where they may be headed. Social work students (as well as practitioners and faculty) who become frustrated with the policy process, or the prospect of political engagement, need to understand the grave stakes involved. They should also be aware that, given the right tools, this new social and political era offers opportunities for policy practice and advocacy to those who understand how to navigate the terrain. In this section, I detail some of the important implications of the content included in this book for faculty who teach social policy and other curricula and current social work students, as well as practitioners and allies for social justice policies.

Implications for Social Work Educators and Students

Related to social work education at all practice levels, metaphors may play an important role in how students come to perceive various families, work groups, neighborhoods, and communities and thus how (or whether) people respond to their needs through advocacy. In human behavior courses, metaphors might be a useful way of conceptualizing human development and the differing views of non-normative development. Metaphor deconstruction may also be a fruitful and unusual area of content analysis in research courses, especially pertaining to the images that are put forth of the profession, specific marginalized groups, or the various social problems with which the profession deals. Thematic metaphor analyses (Barry et al., 2009; Beckett, 2003; Cunningham-Parmeter, 2011; Dodge, 2008; Nicolas & Skinner, 2012) may be used in research classes as exemplars of such scholarship from which students can draw.

Metaphor analysis should especially become a staple of diversity and related areas of study (women's or African American studies, disability courses, classes based on immigrant or refugee issues, and so forth). Faculty should provide an overview of the historical development of specific pejorative themes as well as their contemporary usage, drawing on sources such as Bosmajian (1983), Brennan (1995), Gambrill (2012), Haslam (2006), and Keen (1986), among others. Primary source documents from eras that are characterized by high fear or anger against specific groups can be accessed, and students should be required to analyze the important themes that arise. Reading primary documents written by advocates of restriction or control during a particular alarm period might give students a much better feel for why rationales for control were widely embraced than would simply reading secondary analyses of such events. Students should be encouraged to locate and consider the role that specific dehumanizing metaphors played in fostering public fear and anger against the group in question, and discussion can address possible contemporary correlates.

Immigration in particular is a pressing social issue, and numerous publications have provided metaphoric analyses of immigration that students could use as examples of research on metaphor deconstruction and its importance (Cisneros, 2008; Cunningham-Parmeter, 2011; J. Lederer, 2013; O'Brien, 2003; Park & Kemp, 2006; Santa Ana, 2002). Various forms of contemporary media (newspaper or other mass circulation articles, blogs, speeches, professional journal articles, editorial or other cartoons, advertising images, and so forth) can also serve as useful content vehicles for research projects that require students to analyze metaphor themes. Students may be asked to look for and bring in examples of pejorative metaphor themes that they come across in the news or popular culture, and these examples can be used as a starting point for class discussions on the topic.

Faculty in social work and related professions who teach social policy should find ways to incorporate metaphor components in their syllabi, and they may even require students to include sections in policy papers or lobbying activities on the perceptual images and media and stakeholder framing of specific client groups. Students need to understand that specific policies are often developed with a stereotypic image of the client or client group in mind (Schneider, Ingram, & deLeon, 2014), and they should be made aware of the framing–policy–service pipeline. Denigrating stereotypes often have an extremely long shelf life because the metaphors that are intrinsically related to those stereotypes become cultural touchstones or connect with important cultural myths or values (Goff et al., 2008). Moreover, these images are often transplanted from one vulnerable population to another across time periods.

Policy courses should include content on why specific images or issue framings have "stickiness," to use a term popularized by Malcolm Gladwell (2002), and why others do not. As noted, it is also important to identify the various ways in which stakeholders attempt to keep a preferred framing of an issue in the public eye, often by exploiting tragedies or particularly egregious cases or events or by highlighting particular members of a targeted group and presenting them as representative exemplars of the group norm.

Instructors might use visual means of information dispersal (television shows and movies, Web-based sources, documentaries, political commercials, and so forth) as a means of analyzing denigrating linguistic and conceptual metaphors. Students should be challenged not only to identify these metaphors, but also to understand the reasons behind such images: whether they support or counter existing stereotypes of the population, whether there is a factual basis for the depictions, what form of policy might reasonably be expected to result from such images, and, again, which stakeholder benefits might accrue from such policies.

Policy debates, press conferences, and convention speeches often provide an interesting opportunity for students to study political narrative and image making. During election years, I have developed real-time Blackboard discussion assignments to have policy students analyze debates while watching them in their home. Students are given a number of issues and questions that they can draw on for discussions as the debate continues, with some of these questions related to the use of metaphors or why specific terms or examples of a problem or group might be used to make a point. Electoral mailings are another interesting source for analysis. It is useful to compare mailings in support of and opposition to a particular candidate and ask relevant questions: How are photographs used or misused, what scare tactics are used, and how is purposefully misleading language used to obscure the truth?

Internet Resources

Finally, faculty can draw on several Internet sites to provide interesting examples of metaphor analysis. GLAAD, for example, provides examples of both positive and negative depictions of members of the lesbian, gay, bisexual, transgender, and queer community. A number of disability sites similarly analyze portrayals of people with physical, sensory, intellectual, or mental disabilities. Considering the expansive information available on the Internet, such sites have been developed in relation to virtually all oppressed or minority populations. The Frameworks Institute's site is particularly helpful in analyzing the framing of social issues. Taking up a number of policy areas of interest to social workers (for example, housing, immigration, substance use), the site provides recommendations for the best means of communicating about policy proposals with political stakeholders (Frameworks Institute, 2018), and it can therefore be very useful to students as they prepare for a lobby day or similar experience.

In short, a wide variety of options are available to provide students with the opportunity to assess and evaluate how the social and policy issues that pertain to the profession are differentially framed by stakeholders with competing agendas. Such opportunities should, I believe, be an important facet of all policy courses within the profession.

Implications for Practitioners and Advocates

As noted in the first chapter, metaphor analysis has a long history in social work treatment, both in providing assistance for gathering client information and in gaining awareness of how clients perceive their situation. It also provides clinicians with a mechanism for focusing on or reframing issues, as well as an option for indirectly approaching sensitive or traumatic subjects. It is incumbent on practitioners that they draw on their knowledge of metaphors to assess macro-level factors that may affect their clients or the social problems on which they focus. Clinicians who have experience with metaphor analysis should lend their expertise to social work classes, and not just to practice courses. Conceptual connections between micro- and macro-based metaphor analysis should be fostered in both education programs and agencies.

Although many practitioners have been introduced to policy advocacy and its importance to the profession, too many withdraw from macro-level engagement once they are in practice. G. Miller and Fox (1999) discussed the importance of building connections between scholars and practitioners, and they particularly focused on the importance of working together to understand the social construction of problems and groups. Although the researcher–practitioner divide has been a long-standing concern of social work, it is primarily discussed in relation to the connection (or lack thereof) between scholarly research and micro- or meso-based practice. The divide also occurs in relation to social policy. G. Miller and Fox alluded to the fact that the real-world activities of social workers provide an important contextual milieu within which scholars can assess their own assumptions regarding problem or individual framing, stakeholder and power relationships, and other factors that have an impact on clients at both the agency and policy levels.

Practitioners and agency administrators should develop and maintain relationships with local legislators and be aware of the important policymakers, especially at the state level, who affect their particular areas. Although this seems to be simple common sense, as noted previously, agencies too often begin engaging politically when they are in trouble or have dire need. Although politics may be viewed as driven by money, which agencies cannot spare, it is also driven by relationships, at which agency personnel should be experts. Most politicians are social creatures and in general respond more readily to those with whom they have developed a close connection.

One possible means by which greater coordination in advocacy efforts can be developed is by having academic programs connect their lobby day or other policy activities to agencies and alumni, which I assume some programs have already done. Students and practitioners can work in small groups toward a common policy goal. Such a partnership can serve to augment bridge building in terms of both connecting micro- and macro-level metaphor analysis and closing the scholar–practitioner gap that exists in policy analysis. Many former students who engaged in lobby day activities could be energized by continued involvement and serve as experienced mentors for current students.

CONCLUSION

The ability to effectively deconstruct pejorative metaphors is an important precursor to gaining an understanding of the latent rationales that support social control and cultural prejudices, and thus to developing humane public policy options. In fact, it would be difficult to understand how one could effectively engage in policy advocacy without attending to this important facet of policy making. As noted previously, politicians themselves point to the central role of rhetoric in the political arena through their widespread use of metaphors as well as the financial support they provide to rhetorical and image analysts. Social workers need to engage with this arena to advance policy. As Vicki Lens (2005) wrote, "Whether translating research findings for public consumption or arguing for a policy position that reflects social work values, social workers need a range of rhetorical skills so that our voices can be heard and heeded" (p. 231).

As the importance and science of political rhetoric, including metaphors, has evolved, the image-making industry has boomed—pushed along, it should be mentioned, by the vast expansion of new modes of information, especially social media. Because of the need to set forth the image that they are doing something other than manipulating the public, these individuals will normally present themselves in a more acceptable guise. A plethora of media consultants, legislative aides, think-tank staff, industrial and corporate public relations specialists, and other individuals will spend a great deal of time and effort, as well as a massive amount of money, attempting to create and spread their preferred vision of a social problem in ways that are both easily digestible by the general public and highly profitable for their employers or careers. Because policy analysis is impossible without considering important stakeholder groups, social workers need to see these individuals as strategic players in the political drama, and what they do affects everyone. Social workers becoming heavily involved further down the policy road (for example, attempting to assist with the development, implementation, evaluation, and revision of policies) may do little good if the basic framing of issues and groups is left to others, because this framing forms the essential foundation on which a policy structure is built.

In an era in which anything candidates do not like can be called fake news and when even fact checkers are often biased, people may have a degree of cynicism that is difficult to overcome. In an atmosphere increasingly focused on childish insults and schoolyard taunts (feminazis, libtards, snowflakes, and so forth) that serve only to solidify the barriers that keep people apart, social workers need to remember that there are modes of thought and practice in social science that, as in the natural sciences, can lead all closer to the truth. The recent resurgence of anti-intellectualism allows stakeholders to call into question even hard science data that do not fit their political and economic agendas well, so this is an uphill battle. It is, however, a battle that is worthy of a good fight on the part of social workers who are still interested in the importance of critical thinking and an honest appraisal of difficult issues and who comprehend how much the profession stands to lose by not engaging in such a battle, knowing the tremendous impact it may have on the profession, its clients, and the cause of social justice.

REFERENCES

Abromovitz, M. (2005). The largely untold story of welfare reform and the human services. *Social Work, 50*, 175–186.

Adams, G. D., & Cantor, R. (2001). Risk, stigma, and property value—What are people afraid of? In F. Flynn, P. Slovic, & H. Kunreuther (Eds.), *Risk, media, and stigma: Understanding public challenges to modern science and technology* (pp. 175–185). London: Earthscan.

Adams, M. V. (1997). Metaphors in psychoanalytic theory and therapy. *Clinical Social Work Journal, 25*, 27–39.

Adams, S. H. (1908). Guardians of public health. *McClure's Magazine, 31*, 241–252.

Allbritton, D. W. (1995). When metaphors function as schemas: Some cognitive effects of conceptual metaphors. *Metaphor and Symbolic Activity, 10*, 33–46.

Americans with Disabilities Act of 1990, P.L. 101–336, 42 U.S.C. §§ 12101–12213 (2000).

Anderson, B. (2017). The politics of pests: Immigration and the invasive other. *Social Research, 84*, 7–28.

Annas, G. J. (1995). Reframing the debate on health care by replacing our metaphors. *New England Journal of Medicine, 332*, 745–748.

Associated Press. (2015). *Officials: Mom who lost custody kills kids' services worker*. Retrieved from https://www.apnews.com/3a48613490a44effb61e45a0f5b17f39

Ball, M. (2014). The agony of Frank Luntz. *Atlantic*. Retrieved from https://www.theatlantic.com/politics/archive/2014/01/the-agony-of-frank-luntz/282766/

Bancroft, K. H. (2012). Zones of exclusion: Urban spatial policies, social justice, and social services. *Journal of Sociology and Social Welfare, 39*, 63–84.

Barry, C. L., Brescoll, V. L., Brownell, K. D., & Schlesinger, M. (2009). Obesity metaphors: How beliefs about the causes of obesity affect support for public policy. *Milbank Quarterly, 87*, 7–47.

Barson, M., & Heller, S. (2001). *Red scared! The commie menace in propaganda and popular culture.* San Francisco: Chronicle Books.

Bauman, Z. (1997). *Postmodernity and its discontents.* New York: New York University Press.

Beck, R. (2011). *Unclean: Meditations on purity, hospitality, and mortality.* Eugene, OR: Cascade Books.

Beckett, C. (2003). The language of siege: Military metaphors in the spoken language of social work. *British Journal of Social Work, 33*, 625–639.

Ben-Amitay, G., Buchbinder, E., & Toren, P. (2015). Understanding sexual revictimization of women through metaphors: A qualitative research. *Journal of Aggression, Maltreatment and Trauma, 24*, 914–931.

Bendetsen, K. R. (1942). The Japanese evacuation. *Vital Speeches of the Day, 8*, 541–544.

Bennett, J. (2009). *Banning queer blood: Rhetorics of citizenship, contagion, and resistance.* Tuscaloosa: University of Alabama Press.

Bennetts, L. (1993). Letter from Las Vegas: Jerry vs. the kids. *Vanity Fair, 56*, 82–98.

Berger, M. A. (2011). *Seeing through race: A reinterpretation of civil rights photography.* Berkeley: University of California Press.

Berke, R. L. (2000, September 12). The 2000 campaign: The ad campaign; Democrats see, and smell, rats in G.O.P. ad. *New York Times.* Retrieved from http://www.nytimes.com/2000/09/12/us/the-2000-campaign-the-ad-campaign-democrats-see-and-smell-rats-in-gop-ad.html

Best, J. (Ed.). (1995). *Images of issues: Typifying contemporary social problems* (2nd ed.). New York: Aldine de Gruyter.

Bethell, T. (1993, August 23). They had a dream: The challenge of welfare reform. *National Review,* pp. 31–37.

Bettelheim, B. (1976). *The uses of enchantment: The meaning and importance of fairy tales.* New York: Alfred A. Knopf.

Biale, D. (2007). *Blood and belief. The circulation of a symbol between Jews and Christians.* Berkeley: University of California Press.

Bishop, B. (2008). *The big sort: Why the clustering of like-minded America is tearing us apart.* Boston: Mariner Books.

Black, E. (2003). *War against the weak: Eugenics and America's campaign to create a master race.* New York: Four Walls Eight Windows.

Blatt, B. (1970). *Exodus from pandemonium.* Boston: Allyn & Bacon.

Bock, G. (1983). Racism and sexism in Nazi Germany, motherhood, compulsory sterilization and the state. *Signs: Journal of Women in Culture and Society, 8,* 400–421.

Bogdan, R. (1988). *Freak show: Presenting human oddities for amusement and profit.* Chicago: University of Chicago Press.

Boone, C. K. (1988). Bad axioms in genetic engineering. *Hastings Center Report, 18*(4), 9–17.

Bosmajian, H. A. (1983). *The language of oppression.* Lanham, MD: University Press of America.

Bougher, D. (2012). The case for metaphor in political reasoning and cognition. *Political Psychology, 33,* 145–163.

Boysen, G. A. (2009). A review of experimental studies of explicit and implicit bias among counselors. *Journal of Multicultural Counseling and Development, 37,* 240–249.

Brennan, W. (1995). *Dehumanizing the vulnerable: When word games take lives.* Chicago: Loyola University Press.

Browning, T. (Producer), & Browning, T. (Director). (1932). *Freaks* [Motion picture]. United States: Metro-Goldwin-Mayer.

Burke, A. C. (1992). Between entitlement and control: Dimensions of U.S. drug control policy. *Social Service Review, 66,* 571–581.

Burleigh, M. (1994). *Death and deliverance: "Euthanasia" in Germany 1900–1945.* New York: Cambridge University Press.

Burr, V. (1995). *An introduction to social constructionism.* Florence, KY: Taylor & Francis/Routledge.

Campbell, J. (2008). *The hero with a thousand faces* (3rd ed.). Novato, CA: New World Library.

Cannon, C. J. (1923). Selecting citizens. *North American Review, 217,* 325–333.

Carroll, C. (1900). *The Negro a beast.* Miami: Mnemosyne.

Cavalieri, P., & Singer, P. (Eds.). (1993). *The Great Ape Project: Equality beyond humanity.* New York: St. Martin's Green.

Chapman, H. A., & Anderson, A. K. (2013). Things rank and gross in nature: A review and synthesis of moral disgust. *Psychological Bulletin, 139,* 300–327.

Charteris-Black, J. (2009). Metaphor and political communication. In A. Musolff & J. Zinken (Eds.), *Metaphor and discourse* (pp. 97–115). Basingstoke, England: Palgrave Macmillan.

Charteris-Black, J. (2011). *Politicians and rhetoric: The persuasive power of rhetoric* (2nd ed.). Basingstoke, England: Palgrave Macmillan.

Chomsky, A. (2014). *Undocumented: How immigration became illegal.* Boston: Beacon Press.

Church League of America/Edgar Bundy Ministries. (1961). *A manual for survival (a counter-subversive study course).* Wheaton, IL: Church League of America.

Cisneros, J. D. (2008). Contaminated communities: The metaphor of "immigrant as pollutant" in media representations of immigration. *Rhetoric and Public Affairs, 11*, 569–602.

Civil rights-public accommodations: Hearings before the Committee on Commerce, U.S. Senate, 88th Cong. 20 (1963).

Clark, C. (1987). Sympathy biography and sympathy margin. *American Journal of Sociology, 93*, 290–321.

Clark, C. (1998). *Misery and company: Sympathy in everyday life.* Chicago: University of Chicago Press.

Combs, G., & Freedman, J. (1990). *Symbol, story and ceremony: Using metaphor in individual and family therapy.* New York: W. W. Norton.

Comstock, A. P. (1912). Chicago housing conditions, VI: The problem of the Negro. *American Journal of Sociology, 18*, 241–257.

Council on Social Work Education. (2015). *Educational policy and accreditation standards.* Washington, DC: Author.

Crenshaw, D. (2006). Neuroscience and trauma treatment: Implications for creative arts therapists. In L. Cary (Ed.), *Expressive and creative arts methods for trauma survivors* (pp. 21–38). London: Jessica Kingsley.

Crews, J. A., & Hill, N. R. (2005). Diagnosis in marriage and family counseling: An ethical double bind. *Family Journal: Counseling and Therapy for Couples and Families, 13*, 63–66.

Cunningham-Parmeter, K. (2011). Alien language: Immigration metaphors and the jurisprudence of otherness. *Fordham Law Review, 79*, 1545–1598.

Dannemeyer, W. (1989). *Shadow in the land: Homosexuality in America.* San Francisco: Ignatius Press.

Davis, C. J. (2002). Contagion as metaphor. *American Literary History, 14*, 828–836.

De Landtsheer, C. (1994). The language of prosperity and crisis: A case study in political semantics. *Politics and the Individual, 4*(2), 63–83.

Deutsch, N. (2009). *Inventing America's worst family: Eugenics, Islam and the rise and fall of the Tribe of Ishmael*. Berkeley: University of California Press.

De Vos, G. A., & Suárez-Orozco, M. M. (1990). Sacrifice and the experience of power. In G. A. De Vos & M. M. Suárez-Orozco (Eds.), *Status inequality: The self in culture* (pp. 120–147). Newbury Park, CA: Sage Publications.

Dodge, K. A. (2008). Framing public policy and prevention of chronic violence in American youths. *American Psychologist, 63*, 573–590.

Dolmage, J. (2011, Winter). Disabled upon arrival: The rhetorical construction of disability and race at Ellis Island. *Cultural Critique, 77*, 24–69.

Douglas, M. (1984). *Purity and danger: An analysis of the concepts of pollution and taboo* (Rev. ed.). London: Ark Paperbacks.

Duffy, J. (1992). *The Sanitarians: A history of American public health*. Urbana: University of Illinois Press.

Duffy, T. K. (2001). White gloves and cracked vases: How metaphors help group workers construct new perspectives and responses. *Social Work with Groups, 24*, 89–99.

DuPuis, E. M. (2015). *Dangerous digestion: The politics of American dietary advice*. Berkeley: University of California Press.

Ellis, W. T. (1923). Americans on guard. *Saturday Evening Post, 196*, 23, 80, 83, 86.

Ellwood, W. N. (1995). Declaring war on the home front: Metaphor, presidents, and the war on drugs. *Metaphor and Symbolic Activity, 10*, 93–114.

End of the "melting-pot" theory. (1924). *Literary Digest, 81*(10), 14–15.

Ewen, E., & Ewen, S. (2006). *Typecasting, on the arts and sciences of human inequality: A history of dominant ideas*. New York: Seven Stories Press.

Fiedler, L. (1978). *Freaks: Myths and images of the secret self*. New York: Touchstone Books.

Fisher, R. (1994). *Let the people decide: Neighborhood organizing in America*. New York: Twayne.

Forte, J. A. (2009). Teaching human development: Current theoretical deficits and a theory-enriched "models, metaphors, and maps" remedy. *Journal of Human Behavior in the Social Environment, 19*, 932–954.

Foucault, M. (1965). *Madness and civilization* (R. Howard, Trans.). New York: Vintage Books.

Fox, R. (1989). What is meta for? *Clinical Social Work Journal, 17*, 233–244.

Frameworks Institute. (2018). *About us.* Retrieved from https://www.frameworksinstitute.org/mission.html

Fraser, N. (1989). *Unruly practices: Power, discourse, and gender in contemporary social theory.* Minneapolis: University of Minnesota Press.

Frazier, E. (1923). Our foreign cities—Pittsburgh. *Saturday Evening Post, 195*, 23, 85, 88, 91, 94.

Freire, P. (1970). *Pedagogy of the oppressed* (M. B. Ramos, Trans.). New York: Herder & Herder.

Gambrill, E. (2012). *Propaganda in the helping professions.* New York: Oxford University Press.

Garland-Thomson, R. (2001). Seeing the disabled: Visual rhetorics of disability in popular photography. In P. K. Longmore & L. Umansky (Eds.), *The new disability history: American perspectives* (pp. 335–374). New York: New York University Press.

Geary, J. (2012). *I is an other: The secret life of metaphor and how it shapes the way we see the world.* New York: Harper Perennial.

Gelb, S. A. (1995). The beast in man: Degeneration and mental retardation, 1900–1920. *Mental Retardation, 33*(1), 1–9.

Gergen, K. J. (1999). *An invitation to social construction.* London: Sage Publications.

Giesen, J. C. (2011). *Boll weevil blues: Cotton, myth, and power in the American South.* Chicago: University of Chicago Press.

Gilman, S. (1984). Jews and mental illness: Medical metaphors, anti-Semitism, and the Jewish response. *Journal of the History of the Behavioral Sciences, 20*, 150–159.

Gilman, S. (1988). *Disease and representation: Images of illness from madness to AIDS.* Ithaca, NY: Cornell University Press.

Ginsberg, L. (1996). *Understanding social problems, policies, and programs* (2nd ed.). Columbia: University of South Carolina Press.

Girard, R. (1989). *The scapegoat* (Y. Freccero, Trans.). Baltimore: Johns Hopkins University Press.

Gladwell, M. (2002). *The tipping point: How little things can make a big difference* (2nd ed.). New York: Little, Brown.

Glassner, B. (1999). *The culture of fear: Why Americans are afraid of the wrong things.* New York: Basic Books.

Goatly, A. (2007). *Washing the brain-metaphor and hidden ideology.* Amsterdam: John Benjamins.

Goddard, H. H. (2012, March 2). The basis for state policy. *The Survey, 27*, 1852–1854.

Goebbels, J. (1932, January). What Hitler will do. *Living Age,* 388–395.

Goff, P. A., Eberhardt, J. L., Williams, M. J., & Jackson, M. C. (2008). Less than human: Implicit knowledge, historical dehumanization, and contemporary consequences. *Journal of Personality and Social Psychology, 94*, 292–306.

Goffman, E. (1959). *The presentation of self in everyday life*. Garden City, NY: Anchor.

Goffman, E. (1961). *Asylums: Essays on the social situation of mental patients and other inmates*. Garden City, NY: Anchor.

Goffman, E. (1963). *Stigma: Notes on the management of spoiled identity*. Englewood Cliffs, NJ: Prentice-Hall.

Goldhagen, D. J. (2009). *Worse than war: Genocide, eliminationism and the ongoing assault on humanity*. New York: Public Affairs.

Goldstein, H. (1999). The limits and art of understanding in social work practice. *Families in Society, 80*, 385–395.

Goodwin, M., & Chemerinsky, E. (2016). No immunity: Race, class, and civil liberties in times of health crisis. *Harvard Law Review, 129*, 956–996.

Gorin, S. H., & Moniz, C. (2017). Affordable Care Act update: Can the Republicans really reform it? [Editorial]. *Health & Social Work, 42*, 69–70.

Gosney, E. S., & Popenoe, P. (1929). *Sterilization for human betterment*. New York: Macmillan.

Gould, S. J. (1980). *The panda's thumb*. New York: W. W. Norton.

Gould, S. J. (1981). *The mismeasure of man*. New York: W. W. Norton.

Gould, S. J. (1995). *Dinosaur in a haystack*. New York: Harmony Books.

Greenbaum, S., Hathaway, W., Rodriguez, C., Spalding, A., & Ward, B. (2008). Deconcentration and social capital: Contradictions of a poverty alleviation policy. *Journal of Poverty, 12*, 201–228.

Gregg, R. B. (2004). Embodied meaning in American public discourse during the Cold War. In F. A. Beer & C. De Landtsheer (Eds.), *Metaphorical world politics* (pp. 59–73). East Lansing: Michigan State University Press.

Gring-Pemble, L. M. (2003). *Grim fairy tales: The rhetorical construction of American welfare policy*. Westport, CT: Praeger.

Gross, A. J. (2010). *What blood won't tell: A history of race on trial in America*. Cambridge, MA: Harvard University Press.

Guarding the gates against undesirables. (1924). *Current Opinion, 76*, 400–401.

Gwyn, R. (1999). "Captain of my own ship": Metaphor and the discourse of chronic illness. In L. Cameron & G. Low (Eds.), *Researching and applying metaphor* (pp. 203–220). Cambridge, MA: Cambridge University Press.

Haidt, J. (2012). *The righteous mind: Why good people are divided by politics and religion.* New York: Random House.

Hale, G. E. (1998). *Making whiteness: The culture of segregation in the South, 1890–1940.* New York: Vintage.

Haley, J. (1973). *Uncommon therapy: The psychiatric techniques of Milton H. Erickson, M.D.* New York: W. W. Norton.

Hall, W. J., Chapman, M. V., Lee, K. M., Merino, Y. M., Thomas, T. W., Payne, B. K., et al. (2015). Implicit racial/ethnic bias among health care professionals and its influence on health care outcomes: A systematic review. *American Journal of Public Health, 105*, e60–e76.

Haller, J. S., Jr. (1971). *Outcasts from evolution: Scientific attitudes of racial inferiority, 1859–1900.* Carbondale: Southern Illinois University Press.

Harper, I., & Raman, P. (2008). Less than human? Diaspora, disease and the question of citizenship. *International Migration, 46*(5), 3–26.

Harrington, A. (1995). Metaphoric connections: Holistic science in the shadow of the Third Reich. *Social Research, 62*, 357–385.

Harris, L. T., & Fiske, S. T. (2006). Dehumanizing the lowest of the low: Neuroimaging responses to extreme out-groups. *Psychological Science, 17*, 847–853.

Haslam, N. (2006). Dehumanization: An integrative review. *Personality and Social Psychology Review, 10*, 252–264.

Haslam, N., Loughnan, S., & Sun, P. (2011). Beastly: What makes animal metaphors offensive? *Journal of Language and Social Psychology, 30*, 311–325.

Hauser, D. J., & Schwarz, N. (2015). The war on prevention: Bellicose cancer metaphors hurt (some) prevention intentions. *Personality and Social Psychology Bulletin, 41*, 66–77.

Herzogenrath, B. (2010). *An American body/politic: A Deleuzian approach.* Lebanon, NH: Dartmouth College Press.

Hillel, M., & Henry, C. (1976). *Of pure blood* (E. Mossbacher, Trans.). New York: McGraw-Hill.

Hitler, A. (1971). *Mein kampf* [My fight] (R. Manheim, Trans.). Boston: Houghton Mifflin. (Original work published 1925)

References

Hogan, J. (2009). *Gender, race and national identity: Nations of flesh and blood*. New York: Routledge.

Hoover, H. (1954, September 1). The protection of freedom: A constant battle against the "abuse of power." *Vital Speeches of the Day, 20*, 679–682.

Horsman, R. (1981). *Race and manifest destiny: The origins of American racial Anglo Saxonism*. Cambridge, MA: Harvard University Press.

Inda, J. X. (2000). Foreign bodies: Migrants, parasites, and the pathological nation. *Discourse, 22*, 46–62.

Indurkhya, B. (1992). *Metaphor and cognition: An interactionist approach*. Dordrecht, the Netherlands: Kluwer Academic.

The international Jew: The world's foremost problem (4 vols.). (1920). Dearborn, MI: Dearborn Publishing.

Jansson, B. S. (2001). *The reluctant welfare state: American social welfare policies—Past, present and future* (4th ed.). Belmont, CA: Brooks/Cole.

Jecker, N. S. (2014). Against a duty to die. *AMA Journal of Ethics, 16*(5), 390–394. Retrieved from http://journalofethics.ama-assn.org/2014/05/oped1-1405.html

Jung, C. G. (1964). *Man and his symbols*. New York: Dell.

Keen, S. (1986). *Faces of the enemy: Reflections of the hostile imagination*. San Francisco: Harper & Row.

Keller, H. (1915, December 18). Physicians' juries for defective babies [Letter to the Editor]. *New Republic*, 173–174.

Kennan, G. (1953, August 24). The nature of the challenge. *New Republic*, 9–12.

Kennedy, A. C. (2008). Eugenics, "degenerate girls," and social workers during the Progressive Era. *Affilia, 23*, 22–37.

Kingdon, J. (2003). *Agendas, alternatives, and public policies* (2nd ed.). New York: Longman.

Kirk, S. A., & Kutchins, H. (1992). *The selling of DSM: The rhetoric of science in psychiatry*. New York: Aldine de Gruyter.

Kopp, R. R. (1995). *Metaphor therapy: Using client-generated metaphors in psychotherapy*. New York: Brunner/Mazel.

Kövecses, Z. (2010). *Metaphor: A practical introduction* (2nd ed.). New York: Oxford University Press.

Kraut, A. M. (1994). *Silent travelers: Germs, genes and the "immigrant menace."* New York: Basic Books.

Kühl, S. (1994). *The Nazi connection: Eugenics: American racism, and German National Socialism*. New York: Oxford University Press.

Lakoff, G. (1995). Metaphor, morality and politics: Or, why conservatives have left liberals in the dust. *Social Research, 62*, 177–213.

Lakoff, G. (1996). *Moral politics: What conservatives know that liberals don't.* Chicago: University of Chicago Press.

Lakoff, G. (2008). *The political mind.* New York: Viking.

Lakoff, G. (2014). *Don't think of an elephant: Know your values and frame the debate.* White River Junction, VT: Chelsea Green Publishing.

Landau, M. J., & Keefer, L. A. (2014). This is like that: Metaphors in public discourse shape attitudes. *Social and Personality Psychology Compass, 8*, 463–473.

Landau, M. J., Keefer, L. A., & Rothschild, Z. K. (2014). Epistemic motives moderate the effect of metaphoric framing on attitudes. *Journal of Experimental Social Psychology, 53*, 125–138.

Landau, M. J., Sullivan, D., & Greenberg, J. (2009). Evidence that self-relevant motives and metaphoric framing interact to influence political and social attitudes. *Psychological Science, 20*, 1421–1427.

Lane, H. (1992). *Mask of benevolence: Disabling the deaf community.* New York: Alfred A. Knopf.

LaPan, A., & Platt, T. (2005). "To stem the tide of degeneracy": The eugenic impulse in social work. In S. A. Kirk (Ed.), *Mental disorders in the social environment* (pp. 139–164). New York: Columbia University Press.

Lawrence, D. (1960, July 25). Is war the only way? *U.S. News & World Report, 51*, 112.

Leary, D. E. (1990). Psyche's muse: The role of metaphor in the history of psychology. In D. E. Leary (Ed.), *Metaphors in the history of psychology* (pp. 1–78). Cambridge, England: Cambridge University Press.

Lederer, J. (2013). "Anchor baby": A conceptual explanation for pejoration. *Journal of Pragmatics, 57*, 248–266.

Lederer, S. E. (2008). *Flesh and blood: Organ transplantation and blood transfusion in twentieth-century America.* New York: Oxford University Press.

Lee, S.W.S., & Schwartz, N. (2013). Metaphor in judgment and decision making. In M. J. Landau, M. D. Robinson, & B. P. Meier (Eds.), *The power of metaphor: Examining its influence on social life* (pp. 85–108). Washington, DC: American Psychological Association.

Lennox, W. G. (1938). Should they live? *American Scholar, 13*, 454–466.

Lens, V. (2005). Advocacy and argumentation in the public arena: A guide for social workers. *Social Work, 50*, 231–238.

Levin, M. B. (1971). *Political hysteria in America.* New York: Basic Books.

Levine, D. N. (1995). The organism metaphor in sociology. *Social Research, 62*, 239–265.

Lewis, J. (1990, September 2). If I had muscular dystrophy. *Parade Magazine,* 4–6.

Lindhorst, D. M. (2002). Federalism and social justice: Implications for social work. *Social Work, 47*, 201–208.

Linton, S. (2007). *My body politic: A memoir.* Ann Arbor: University of Michigan Press.

Livneh, H. (1991). On the origin of negative attitudes toward people with disabilities. In R. P. Marinelli & A. E. Dell Orto (Eds.), *The psychological and social impact of disability* (pp. 181–196). New York: Springer.

Lombroso, C. (1968). *Crime: Its causes and remedies* (reprint; H. P. Horton, Trans.). Montclair, NJ: Patterson Smith. (Original work published 1911)

Longmore, P. K. (2003). *Why I burned my book and other essays on disability.* Philadelphia: Temple University Press.

Longmore, P. K., & Umansky L. (Eds.). (2001). *The new disability history: American perspectives.* New York: New York University Press.

Loseke, D. R. (2003). *Thinking about social problems: An introduction to constructionist perspectives* (2nd ed.). New York: Aldine de Gruyter.

Lott, T. L. (1999). *The invention of race: Black culture and the politics of representation.* Malden, MA: Blackwell.

Loue, S. (2008). *The transformative power of metaphor in therapy.* New York: Springer.

Lovejoy, A. O. (1966). *The great chain of being.* Cambridge, MA: Harvard University Press.

Lowenthal, L., & Guterman, N. (1970). *Prophets of deceit: A study of techniques of the American agitator* (reprint ed.). Palo Alto, CA: Pacific Books. (Original work published 1949)

Lowney, K. S., & Best, J. (1995). Stalking strangers and lovers: Changing media typifications of a new crime problem. In J. Best (Ed.), *Images of issues: Typifying contemporary social problems* (2nd ed., pp. 33–57). New York: Aldine de Gruyter.

Luntz, F. (2007). *Words that work: It's not what you say, it's what people hear.* New York: MFJ Books.

Lyddon, W. J., Clay, A. L., & Sparks, C. L. (2001). Metaphor and change in counseling. *Journal of Counseling and Development, 79*, 269–274.

Lyness, K., & Thomas, V. (1995). Fitting a square peg in a square hole: Using metaphor in narrative therapy. *Contemporary Family Therapy, 17*, 127–142.

Maass, A., Suitner, C., & Arcuri, L. (2014). The role of metaphors in intergroup relations. In M. J. Landau, M. D. Robinson, & B. P. Meier (Eds.), *The power of metaphor: Examining its influence on social life* (pp. 153–177). Washington, DC: American Psychological Association.

Mackelprang, R. W., & Salsgiver, R. O. (2015). *Disability: A diversity model approach in human service practice* (3rd ed.). Chicago: Lyceum Books.

Markel, H., & Stern, A. M. (2002). The foreignness of germs: The persistent association of immigrants and disease in American society. *Milbank Quarterly, 80*, 757–788.

Marson, S. M., & Powell, R. M. (2014). Goffman and the infantilization of elderly persons: A theory in development. *Journal of Sociology and Social Welfare, 41*, 143–158.

Maudsley, H. (1898). *Responsibility in mental disease.* New York: Appleton.

Mayer, R., & Weingart, B. (2012). Discursive contamination: Terrorism, the body politic, and the virus as trope. In M. M. Hampf & M. Snyder-Körber (Eds.), *Machine: Bodies, genders, technologies* (pp. 137–156). Heidelberg, Germany: Universitätsverlag.

McBeth, M. K., Jones, M. D., & Shanahan, E. A. (2014). The narrative policy framework. In P. A. Sabatier & C. M. Weible (Eds.), *Theories of the policy process* (3rd ed., pp. 225–266). Boulder, CO: Westview Press.

McCarthy, J. (1952). *McCarthyism: The fight for America.* Old Greenwich, CT: Devin-Adair.

McKim, W. D. (1901). *Heredity and human progress.* New York: Putnam.

McWilliams, C. (1935, June 26). Once again the "yellow peril." *Nation, 140*, 735–736.

Memorial of Miss Dix. (1863). In *Reports of the Illinois State Hospital for the Insane.* Chicago: F. Fulton.

Metrick-Chen, L. (2012). *Collecting objects/excluding people: Chinese subjects and American visual culture.* Albany: SUNY Press.

Metzl, J. M. (2009). *The protest psychosis: How schizophrenia became a black disease.* Boston: Beacon Press.

Miller, G., & Fox, K. J. (1999). Learning from sociological practice: The case of applied constructionism. *American Sociologist, 30*, 54–73.

Miller, S. C. (1969). *The unwelcome immigrant: The American image of the Chinese, 1785–1882.* Berkeley: University of California Press.

Miller, W. I. (1997). *The anatomy of disgust*. Cambridge, MA: Harvard University Press.

Miller, W. L. (1980). Casework and the medical metaphor. *Social Work, 25*, 281–285.

Mnookin, S. (2011). *The panic virus: The true story behind the vaccine-autism controversy*. New York: Simon & Schuster.

Moran, R., & Gillett, S. (2014). Twenty first century eugenics? A case study about the Merton test. In M. Lavalette & L. Penketh (Eds.), *Race, racism, and social work: Contemporary issues and debates* (pp. 223–241). Bristol, England: Policy Press.

Murdach, A. D. (2006). Rhetoric for direct practice [Points & Viewpoints]. *Social Work, 51*, 365–368.

Musolff, A. (2004). *Metaphor and political discourse: Analogical reasoning in debates about Europe*. Basingstoke, England: Palgrave Macmillan.

Musolff, A. (2007). What role do metaphors play in racial prejudice? The function of anti-Semitic imagery in Hitler's *Mein kampf*. *Patterns of Prejudice, 41*, 21–43.

Musolff, A. (2010). *Metaphor, nation and the Holocaust: The concept of the body politic*. New York: Routledge.

National Association of Social Workers. (2017). *Code of ethics of the National Association of Social Workers*. Retrieved from https://www.socialworkers.org/About/Ethics/Code-of-Ethics/Code-of-Ethics-English

Nelkin, D., & Gilman, S. L. (1988). Placing blame for devastating disease. *Social Research, 55*, 361–378.

Nelkin, D., & Tancredi, L. (1989). *Dangerous diagnostics: The social power of biological information*. New York: Basic Books.

Nicolas, G., & Skinner, A. L. (2012). "That's so gay!": Priming the general negative usage of the word *gay* increases implicit anti-gay bias. *Journal of Social Psychology, 152*, 654–658.

Nielsen, K. (2001). Helen Keller and the politics of civic fitness. In P. K. Longmore & L. Umansky (Eds.), *The new disability history: American perspectives* (pp. 268–290). New York: New York University Press.

Noël, L. (1994). *Intolerance: A general survey* (A. Bennett, Trans.). Montreal: McGill-Queen's University Press.

Now a Japanese "peril" in Hawaii. (1925, June 6). *Literary Digest, 85*, 13.

Nussbaum, M. (2004). *Hiding from humanity: Disgust, shame and the law*. Princeton, NJ: Princeton University Press.

Nussbaum, M. (2006). *Frontiers of justice: Disability, nationality, species membership*. Cambridge, MA: Belknap Press.

O'Brien, G. V. (1999). Protecting the social body: The use of the organism metaphor in fighting the "menace of the feeble-minded." *Mental Retardation, 37*, 188–200.

O'Brien, G. V. (2003a). Indigestible food, conquering hordes, and waste materials: Metaphors of immigrants and the early immigration restriction debate in the U.S. *Metaphor and Symbol, 18*(1), 33–47.

O'Brien, G. V. (2003b). People with cognitive disabilities: The argument from marginal cases and social work ethics. *Social Work, 48*, 331–337.

O'Brien, G. (2004). Rosemary Kennedy: The importance of a historical footnote. *Journal of Family History, 29*, 225–236.

O'Brien, G. V. (2009). Metaphors and the pejorative framing of marginalized groups: Implications for social work education. *Journal of Social Work Education, 45*, 29–46.

O'Brien, G. V. (2010). Social justice implications of the organism metaphor. *Journal of Sociology and Social Welfare, 37*, 95–114.

O'Brien, G. (2011a). Anchors on the ship of progress and weeds in the human garden: Objectivist rhetoric in American eugenic writings. *Disability Studies Quarterly, 31*(3). Retrieved from http://dsq-sds.org/article/view/1668

O'Brien, G. V. (2011b). Eugenics, genetics, and the minority group model of disabilities: Implications for social work advocacy. *Social Work, 56*, 347–354.

O'Brien, G. V. (2013). *Framing the moron: The social construction of feeble-mindedness in the American eugenic era*. Manchester, England: Manchester University Press.

O'Brien, G. V. (2018). *Contagion and the national body: The organism metaphor in American thought*. London: Taylor & Francis/Routledge.

O'Brien, G. V., & Bundy, M. E. (2009). Reaching beyond the "moron": Eugenic control of secondary disability groups. *Journal of Sociology and Social Welfare, 36*, 153–172.

O'Brien, G. V., & Ellegood, C. (2005). The Americans with Disabilities Act: A decision tree for social services administrators. *Social Work, 50*, 271–279.

O'Brien, G. V., & Molinari, A. (2011). Religious metaphors as a justification for eugenic control: A historical analysis. In D. Schumm & M. Stoltzfus (Eds.), *Disability in Judaism, Christianity and Islam:*

Sacred texts, historical traditions and social analysis (pp. 141–165). New York: Palgrave Macmillan.

O'Donnell, V. (2006). The influence of the built environment. In G. S. Jowett & V. O'Donnell (Eds.), *Readings in propaganda and persuasion: New and classic essays* (pp. 213–224). Thousand Oaks, CA: Sage Publications.

Palmer, N. (2002). Reflections on the art of social work practice: A metaphor from the drawing of a swan. *Affilia, 17*, 191–205.

Park, Y. (2008a). Facilitating injustice: Tracing the role of social workers in the World War II internment of Japanese Americans. *Social Service Review, 82*, 447–483.

Park, Y. (2008b). Making refugees: A historical discourse analysis of the construction of the "refugee" in U.S. social work, 1900–1957. *British Journal of Social Work, 38*, 771–787.

Park, Y., & Kemp, S. P. (2006). "Little alien colonies": Representations of immigrants and their neighborhoods in social work discourse, 1875–1924. *Social Service Review, 80*, 705–734.

Patient Protection and Affordable Care Act, P.L. 111–148, 42 U.S.C. §§ 18001–18121 (2010).

Perkins, G. C. (1906). Reasons for continued Chinese exclusion. *North American Review, 183*, 15–23.

Pernick, M. S. (1996). *The black stork: Eugenics and the death of "defective" babies in American medicine and motion pictures since 1915*. New York: Oxford University Press.

Pinker, S. (2008). *The stuff of thought: Language as a window into human nature*. London: Penguin Books.

Pizarro, D. A., & Inbar, Y. (2015). Explaining the influence of disgust on political judgment: A disease-avoidant account. In J. P. Forgas, K. Fiedler, & W. D. Crano (Eds.), *Social psychology and politics* (pp. 163–172). New York: Psychology Press.

Placek, P. J., & Hendershot, G. E. (1974). Public welfare and family planning: An empirical study of the "brood sow" myth. *Social Problems, 21*, 658–673.

Proctor, R. (1988). *Racial hygiene: Medicine under the Nazis*. Cambridge, MA: Harvard University Press.

Quinsaat, S. (2014). Competing news frames and hegemonic discourses in the construction of contemporary immigration and immigrants in the United States. *Mass Communication and Society, 17*, 573–596.

Rafter, N. H. (1988). *White trash: The eugenic family studies, 1877–1919*. Boston: Northeastern University Press.

Reilly, P. R. (1991). *The surgical solution: A history of involuntary sterilization in the United States*. Baltimore: Johns Hopkins University Press.

Rein, M. (1971). Social policy analysis as the interpretation of beliefs. *Journal of the American Institute of Planners, 37*, 297–310.

Reinarman, C., & Levine, H. G. (1995). The crack attack: America's latest drug scare, 1986–1991. In J. Best (Ed.), *Images of issues: Typifying contemporary social problems* (2nd ed., pp. 147–186). New York: Aldine de Gruyter.

Reisfield, G. M., & Wilson, G. R. (2004). Use of metaphor in the discourse on cancer. *Journal of Clinical Oncology, 22*, 4024–4027.

Riley, S. (1999). *Contemporary art therapy with adolescents*. London: Jessica Kingsley.

Ringmar, E. (2008). Metaphor of social order. In T. Carver & J. Pikalo (Eds.), *Political language and metaphor: Interpreting and changing the world* (pp. 57–82). London: Routledge.

Risen, J. L., & Critcher, C. R. (2011). Visceral fit: While in a visceral state, associated states of the world seem more likely. *Journal of Personality and Social Psychology, 100*, 777–793.

Ritvo, H. (1995). Border trouble: Shifting the line between people and other animals. *Social Research, 62*, 481–500.

Roberts, D. (2002). *Shattered bonds: The color of child welfare*. New York: Basic Books.

Roberts, K. (1924, February 2). Slow poison. *Saturday Evening Post, 196*, 8–9, 54, 58.

Robin, C. (2004). *Fear: The history of a political idea*. New York: Oxford University Press.

Rodríguez, I. L. (2009). Of women, bitches, chickens and vixens: Animal metaphors for women in English and Spanish. *Culture, Language and Representation, 7*, 77–100.

Romo, D. D. (2005). *Ringside seat to a revolution*. El Paso, TX: Cinco Puntos Press.

Rosen, M., Clark, G. R., & Kivitz, M. S. (Ed.). (1976). *The history of mental retardation: Volume I*. Baltimore: University Park Press.

Rothman, D. J. (1982). Were Tuskegee and Willowbrook "studies in nature"? *Hastings Center Report, 12*(2), 5–7.

Rowell, C. H. (1913). The Japanese in California. *World's Work, 26*, 196–201.

Rozin, P., Haidt, J., & McCauley, C. (2009). Disgust: The body and soul emotion in the 21st century. In B. O. Olatunji & D. McKay (Eds.), *Disgust and its disorders: Theory, assessment, and treatment implications* (pp. 9–25). Washington, DC: American Psychological Association.

Rozin, P., Markwith, M., & McCauley, C. (1994). Sensitivity to indirect contacts with other persons: AIDS aversion as a composite of aversion to strangers, infection, moral taint, and misfortune. *Journal of Abnormal Psychology, 103*, 495–504.

Russell, E. P. (1996). "Speaking of annihilation": Mobilizing for war against human and insect enemies, 1914–1945. *Journal of American History, 82*, 1505–1529.

Rutten, K., Mottart, A., & Soetaert, R. (2010). Narrative and rhetoric in social work education. *British Journal of Social Work, 40*, 480–495.

Ryan, T. (2014). The moral priority of vulnerability and dependency: Why social work should respect both humans *and* animals. In T. Ryan (Ed.), *Animals in social work: Why and how they matter* (pp. 80–101). Basingstoke, England: Palgrave Macmillan.

Saari, C. (1986). The use of metaphor in therapeutic communication with young adolescents. *Child and Adolescent Social Work, 3*, 15–25.

Sanford, N., & Comstock, C. (Eds). (1971). *Sanctions for evil.* San Francisco: Jossey-Bass.

Santa Ana, O. (2002). *Brown tide rising: Metaphors of Latinos in contemporary American public discourse.* Austin: University of Texas Press.

Sax, B. (2000). *Animals in the Third Reich: Pets, scapegoats, and the Holocaust.* New York: Continuum.

Schneider, A., & Ingram, H. (1993). Social construction of target populations: Implications for politics and policy. *American Political Science Review, 87*, 334–347.

Schneider, A., Ingram, H., & deLeon, P. (2014). Democratic policy design: Social construction of target populations. In P. A. Sabatier & C. M. Weible (Eds.), *Theories of the policy process* (3rd ed., pp. 105–150). Boulder, CO: Westview Press.

Schön, D. A. (1979). Generative metaphor: A perspective on problem-setting in social policy. In A. Ortony (Ed.), *Metaphor and thought* (pp. 254–281). New York: Cambridge University Press.

Semino, E. (2008). *Metaphor in discourse.* Cambridge, England: Cambridge University Press.

Shaffer, E.T.H. (1922, January). A new South: The boll-weevil era. *Atlantic Magazine, 129*, 116–123.
Shapiro, J. (1993). *No pity: People with disabilities forging a new civil rights movement.* New York: Random House.
Shinozuka, J. N. (2013). Deadly perils: Japanese beetles and the pestilential immigrant, 1920s–1930s. *American Quarterly, 65*, 831–852.
Sibley, D. (1995). *Geographies of exclusion: Society and difference in the West.* London: Routledge.
Sidel, R. (2000). The enemy within: The demonization of poor women. *Journal of Sociology and Social Welfare, 27*, 73–83.
Silaški, N. (2013). Animal metaphors and semantic derogation—Do women think differently from men? *Versita, 12*, 319–332.
Singer, P. (1975). *Animal liberation: A new ethics for our treatment of animals.* New York: Avon.
Singer, P. (1994). *Life and death: The collapse of our traditional ethics.* New York: St. Martin's Press.
Smit, C. R. (2003). "Please call now, before it's too late": Spectacle discourse in the Jerry Lewis Muscular Dystrophy Telethon. *Journal of Popular Culture, 36*, 687–703.
Smith, A. M. (2012). *Hideous progeny: Disability, eugenics, and classic horror cinema.* New York: Columbia University Press.
Smith, C. C. (1904, November 19). Helping the Negro to help himself. *Outlook, 78*, 727–730.
Smith, D. L. (2011). *Less than human: Why we demean, enslave and exterminate others.* New York: St. Martin's Press.
Smith, J. D. (1985). *Minds made feeble: The myth and legacy of the Kallikaks.* Austin, TX: Pro-Ed.
Snyder, S. L., & Mitchell, D. T. (2006). *Cultural locations of disability.* Chicago: University of Chicago Press.
Soffer, M., & Ajzenstadt, M. (2010). Stigma and otherness in the Israeli media's mirror representations of illness. *Qualitative Health Research, 20*, 1033–1049.
Sontag, S. (1990). *Illness as metaphor and AIDS and its metaphors.* New York: Anchor Books.
Spandler, H., Roy, A., & Mckeown, M. (2014). Using football metaphor to engage men in therapeutic support. *Journal of Social Work Practice, 28*, 229–245.
Spencer, H. (1904). *The study of sociology.* New York: Appleton.

Statement of Congressman Rankin. 77th Cong., 88 Cong. Rec. 1682 (1942, Feb. 18).

Stein, H. F. (1995). Domestic wars and the militarization of American biomedicine. *Journal of Psychohistory, 22*, 406–416.

Steiner, J. F. (1917). *The Japanese invasion*. Chicago: A. C. McClurg.

Stott, R., Mansell, W., Salkovskis, P., Lavender, A., & Cartwright-Hatton, S. (2010). *Oxford guide to metaphors in CBT: Building cognitive bridges*. Oxford, England: Oxford University Press.

Strausbaugh, J. (2006). *Black like you: Blackface, whiteface, insult and imitation in American popular culture*. New York: Penguin Books.

Strong, D. S. (1941). *Organized anti-Semitism in America: The rise of group prejudice during the decade 1930–1940*. Washington, DC: American Council on Public Affairs.

Sumarah, J. (1989). Metaphors as a means of understanding staff–resident relationships. *Mental Retardation, 27*, 19–23.

Szasz, T. (1963). *Law, liberty and psychiatry*. New York: Collier.

Szasz, T. (1970). *The manufacture of madness: A comparative study of the Inquisition and the mental health movement*. New York: Harper & Row.

Talibinejad, M. R., & Dastjerdi, H. V. (2005). A cross-cultural study of animal metaphors: When owls are not wise! *Metaphor and Symbol, 20*, 133–150.

Thibodeau, P. H., & Boroditsky, L. (2011). Metaphors we think with: The role of metaphor in reasoning. *PLoS One, 6*(2), e16782.

Thibodeau, P. H., Iyiewuare, P. O., & Boroditsky, L. (2015). Metaphors affect reasoning: Measuring effects of metaphor in a dynamic opinion landscape. In *Proceedings of the 37th Annual Meeting of the Cognitive Science Society* (pp. 2374–2379). Austin, TX: Cognitive Science Society. Retrieved from https://mindmodeling.org/cogsci2015/papers/0408/paper0408.pdf

Thomas, L. (2007). Understanding statistics and research through metaphors: Evidence from cognitive science. *Journal of Social Science Research, 34*, 1–14.

Thurston, R. (1935, December 4). The Nazi war on medicine. *New Republic, 84*, 100–102.

Tiffany, F. (1891). *Life of Dorothea Lynde Dix*. Boston: Houghton, Mifflin.

Todoli, J. (2007). Disease metaphors in urban planning. *Critical Approaches to Discourse Analysis across Disciplines, 1*(2), 51–60.

Tomes, N. (1998). *The gospel of germs: Men, women, and the microbe in American life*. Cambridge, MA: Harvard University Press.

Trent, J. W., Jr. (1994). *Inventing the feeble mind: A history of mental retardation in the United States.* Berkeley: University of California Press.

Trent, J. W., Jr. (1998). Defectives at the World's Fair: Constructing disability in 1904. *Remedial and Special Education, 19,* 201–211.

The typhoon—A dramatization of the Yellow Peril. (1912). *Current Literature, 52,* 567–573.

Vallis, R., & Inayatullah, S. (2016). Policy metaphors: From the tuberculosis crusade to the obesity apocalypse. *Futures, 84*(Pt. B), 133–144.

Voss, F., Kennet, J., Wiley, J., & Schooler, T. E. (1992). Experts at debate: The use of metaphor in the U.S. Senate debate on the Gulf Crisis. *Metaphor and Symbolic Activity, 7,* 197–214.

Warne, F. J. (1971). *The immigrant invasion* (reprint ed.). New York: J. S. Ozer. (Original work published 1913)

Washington, H. A. (2006). *Medical apartheid: The dark history of medical experimentation on black Americans from colonial times to the present.* New York: Harlem Moon.

Weinberg, M. (2005). The mother menagerie: Animal metaphors in the social work relationship with young single mothers. *Critical Social Work, 6*(1). Retrieved from http://www1.uwindsor.ca/criticalsocialwork/the-mother-menagerie-animal-metaphors-in-the-social-work-relationship-with-young-single-mothers

Weindling, P. (1989). *Health, race and German politics between national unification and Nazism, 1870–1945.* Cambridge, England: Cambridge University Press.

Weindling, P. (2000). *Epidemics and genocide in Eastern Europe, 1890–1945.* Oxford, England: Oxford University Press.

Whitaker, R. (2002). *Mad in America: Bad science, bad medicine, and the enduring mistreatment of the mentally ill.* New York: Basic Books.

Wickman, S. A., Daniels, M. H., White, L. J., & Fesmire, S. A. (1999). A "primer" in conceptual metaphor for counselors. *Journal of Counseling and Development, 77,* 389–394.

Wiggam, A. E. (1922). *The new Decalogue of science.* Indianapolis: Bobbs-Merrill.

Wilder, A. (2004). Maybe we should just shut up: The body as an important consideration for group work practice. *Social Work with Groups, 27,* 93–112.

Wiley, J. (1990). *Poletown: Community betrayed.* Urbana: University of Illinois Press.

Williams, J. R. (1995). Using story as metaphor, legacy, and therapy. *Contemporary Family Therapy, 19*, 9–16.

Winter, N.J.G. (2008). *Dangerous frames: How ideas about race and gender shape public opinion.* Chicago: University of Chicago Press.

Wolfensberger, W. (1972). *Normalization.* Toronto: National Institute on Mental Retardation.

Wright, D. (2004). Mongols in our midst: John Langdon Down and the ethnic classification of idiocy, 1858–1924. In S. Noll & J. W. Trent Jr. (Eds.), *Mental retardation in America: A historical reader* (pp. 92–115). New York: New York University Press.

Zhong, C., & House, J. (2013). Dirt, pollution, and purity: A metaphoric perspective on morality. In M. J. Landau, M. D. Robinson, & B. P. Meier (Eds.), *The power of metaphor: Examining its influence on social life* (pp. 109–131). Washington, DC: American Psychological Association.

Zuckier, H. (1996). The essential "other" and the Jew: From antisemitism to genocide. *Social Research, 63*, 1110–1152.

Zuñiga, M. E. (1992). Using metaphors in therapy: Dichos and Latino clients. *Social Work, 37*, 55–60.

INDEX

In this index, *n* denotes note.

A

actuarialism, 74–75, 77
advocacy
   for oppressed populations, 9, 14, 32
   policy, 1, 5–6, 15, 42, 44, 46–47, 52, 107–109
   professional, 40, 42–43, 45, 103
Affordable Care Act, 51*n*11, 100–102
African Americans, 35*n*4, 50, 59, 63, 66, 66*n*10, 78, 87, 92*n*10, 94
alarm periods, 33, 57, 104
alien, 51, 87, 91–92
altruistic metaphor, 33, 56, 67–71, 85
Americans with Disabilities Act, 46*n*7, 102
analogies, in therapy, 18
anchor metaphor, 57
anger, 1, 19, 25, 33, 98, 104–105
animalization, 55–56, 56*n*2, 57–66, 65*n*9, 82. *See also* dehumanization
Asian Americans, 76–77, 87. *See also* Chinese Americans; Japanese Americans
autism, 91*n*7

B

Bancroft, Karen, 91*n*8
Bauman, Zygmunt, 73, 90
Beckett, Chris, 23
Berger, Martin, 4
bias, 5, 25–26, 30, 110
body(ies). *See also* organism metaphor
   contagion metaphors and, 11, 29
   fears of intrusion into, 29, 91*n*7
   as metaphor of group functioning, 15
   metaphors across, 20–22
boundaries, metaphors across, 20–22
Brennan, William, 73
Bush, George H. W., 50*n*9, 82*n*2
Bush, George W., 50–51

C

Campbell, Joseph, 20
Carroll, Charles, 59
Chinese Americans, 61, 92*n*10
civil rights movement, 4, 78, 94
claims makers, 53–54
Clark, Candice, 37*n*6
Code of Ethics of the National Association of Social Workers, 44–45
conceptual metaphors, 12–14, 25, 47, 49, 76, 81, 103, 106
confirmation bias, 25–26
contagion metaphors and responses, 13–14, 13*n*3, 26, 28–29, 37, 58–59, 94–96. *See also* body(ies); disease; organism metaphor
crime, 28, 51, 51*n*10, 60, 60*n*6, 82*n*2
crime metaphors, 86–87
cultural competence, 18–19

D

deconstruction
   of language, 3
   metaphors for, of complex issues, 18–22
dehumanization, 27, 31, 33, 38, 57, 79. *See also* animalization

devaluation, 14, 34–36, 59, 65, 72–74, 74n16, 83, 96–97
disabled individuals. *See also* Americans with Disabilities Act; eugenics
  direct experience with, policy development and, 46–47
  euthanization of, 68–69
  fear of, 26
  medical model and, 19
disaster metaphors, 87–88
disease, 10, 12n2, 13, 14n4, 28n2, 89–91. *See also* body(ies); contagion metaphors and responses; organism metaphor
disgust, 25–29, 37
Dix, Dorothea, 45–47, 46n4
Don't Think of an Elephant (Lakoff), 50–51
double binds, 77–79
drug abuse funding, 28

E
embodiment, 21, 29
emotions, as metaphoric vehicles, 25–27, 51
Erickson, Milton, 16
eugenics, 6, 12n2, 32, 34–35, 60, 66, 68–69, 86n5, 88–89

F
Faces of the Enemy (Keen), 3–4
fear, 25–28, 81–83, 98, 107–109
fear-based metaphors, 83–89
floods, 87–88
Ford, Henry, 79n18
framings, 25–26, 28, 30–36, 105
Fraser, Nancy, 54
Freudian psychotherapy, 16–17

G
Ginsberg, Leon, 43
Goebbels, Joseph, 32
Goffman, Erving, 35, 71, 71n13
Goldhagen, Daniel, 30–31
Great Chain of Being, 62
Grim Fairy Tales: The Rhetorical Construction of American Welfare Policy (Gring-Pemble), 49
Gring-Pemble, Lisa, 49

H
health care policy language, 100–103. *See also* policy
Heller, Helen, 68–69, 86
Hitler, Adolf. *See* Nazi Germany
HIV, 11, 14n4, 26, 58, 83, 92–94
homosexuals, 31, 46n6, 86
Hoover, Herbert, 14
Horton, Willie, 82n2
humanity, scale of, 59–60, 62–64

I
image-based metaphors, 17
immigrants, 29, 64, 84, 91–92, 105
infantilization, 38, 55, 63, 70–71
investment, public, 74–75

J
Japanese Americans, 6, 32, 58, 61, 65, 68, 72, 72n14, 78, 84n4, 91
Jews, metaphors with, 13, 13n3, 32, 72. *See also* Nazi Germany
journey metaphor, 19–20

K
Keen, Sam, 3–4, 95
Kennan, George, 94–95
King, Martin Luther, Jr., 78
Kingdon, John, 46–47
Kopp, Richard, 16

L
Lakoff, George, 11, 48–51
Lamm, Richard, 74, 74n15
language, deconstruction of, 3
Lennox, William, 69
Lewis, Jerry, 75, 75n17
Lombroso, Cesare, 60, 86
Longmore, Paul, 74
Loseke, Donileen, 26
Loue, Sana, 16
Luntz, Frank, 48

M
medical model, 19, 75–76
metaphor(s)
  about social work, 23–24
  conceptual, 12–14, 25, 47, 49, 76, 81, 103, 106
  to deconstruct complex issues, 18–22

Index

metaphor(s) *(cont'd)*
　image-based, 17
　with Jews, 13, 13*n*3
　journey, 19–20
　literature review on social work and, 15–16
　origin of term, 9
　overview and importance of, 10–15
　and public image of social work, 36–40
　responses to, 11–12
　in social policy, 47–51
　social policy development and, 14–15
　and social work education, 22–23
　story-based, 17
　in therapy, 16–18
　thought and, 27–30
metaphorical utterances, 9
Metaphor Therapy (Kopp), 16
Metzl, Jonathan, 86–87
Miller, Walter L., 19
Miller, William I., 51, 96*n*14
missing link theme, 59
model minority concept, 76–77, 103

N
natural catastrophe metaphors, 87–88
Nazi Germany, 5–6, 13, 13*n*3, 56, 62*n*7, 65, 68*n*11, 69, 74*n*16, 77, 82, 92*n*10
Negro as a Beast, The (Carroll), 59
Nielsen, Kim, 85–86
Noël, Lise, 67
Nussbaum, Martha, 62

O
Obamacare, 51*n*11, 100–102
obesity, 28
objectification, 55–58, 75–79
object metaphor, 71–76
organism metaphor, 13*n*3, 65, 90–98. *See also* body(ies); contagion metaphors and responses; disease
oversimplification, 50–51

P
parasite metaphor, 10–13, 34, 38, 64–66
Park, Yoosun, 31–32
Patient Protection and Affordable Care Act, 51*n*11, 100–102

policy
　importance of metaphors in, 47–51
　language, 100–103
　selling of, with metaphors, 48–50
　typifications and, 53–54
　war metaphors and, 85–86
policy advocacy, 1, 5–6, 15, 42, 44, 46–47, 52, 107–109
policy development
　case for social worker involvement in, 43–45
　metaphors and, 14–15
policy making, as emotional enterprise, 2
policy-practice connection, 42–47
Politicians and Rhetoric (Charteris-Black), 20
positive metaphors, 76–79
power relationships, 31–32
primes and priming, 27–28, 27*n*1, 29–30, 63
problem setting, 52–53
products, devalued individuals as, 73–74
Protest Psychosis, The (Metzl), 86–87
public image, of social work, 36–40
public investment, 74–75
public relations, 27, 39–40

R
refugees, 32, 66, 84
religious metaphors, 69–70
Republican Party, 48, 100–101
responses, to metaphors, 11–12
Robin, Corey, 82

S
schemas, 25–26
Schön, Donald, 4
Seeing Through Race: A Reinterpretation of Civil Rights Photography (Berger), 4
self-identification, stigma status and, 35, 35*n*4
simplification, 50–51
sinfulness, 29, 69–70
Singer, Peter, 63
social constructionism, metaphoric framing as, 3, 52–54

social control, 32–33, 61
social media, 1, 7, 39, 109
social policy. *See* policy
Sontag, Susan, 10, 89
source domain, 10, 12
space, metaphors across, 20–22
stereotyping, 14, 21, 26, 34–36, 43–44, 44n2, 63–64, 76–78, 97, 105
story-based metaphors, 17
Sumarah, John, 23
syllogisms, 41
sympathy, 37n6, 103

T
target domain, 10–11, 25
Thomas, Leela, 22
thought, metaphors and, 27–30
typifications, 53–54. *See also* stereotyping

U
Unruly Practices (Fraser), 54
utilitarianism, 74–75

V
vaccines, 91n7
Vital Speeches of the Day (Hoover), 14

W
war metaphors, 28, 83–86, 89
water metaphors, 87–88, 88n6
welfare programs, 10–13, 30, 37–39, 49, 64, 70
Works that Work (Luntz), 48
worthiness, 62–64

Z
Zuckier, Henri, 58
Zuñiga, Maria, 18